Mein Kampf

Hitler's Blueprint for Aryan Supremacy

Titles in the
Words That Changed History series include:

Civil Rights

The Declaration of Independence

The Emancipation Proclamation

The King James Bible

The Liberator

The Nuremberg Laws

The Origin of Species

Uncle Tom's Cabin

The U.S. Constitution

Words
THAT
CHANGED
HISTORY

Mein Kampf
Hitler's Blueprint for Aryan Supremacy

by Duane Damon

LUCENT
BOOKS®

THOMSON
™
GALE

San Diego • Detroit • New York • San Francisco • Cleveland
New Haven, Conn. • Waterville, Maine • London • Munich

To my brother John, with affection

On Cover: Hitler (in light uniform) and others salute during
Heroes' Memorial Day services at the state opera theater in Berlin.

LIBRARY OF CONGRESS CATALOGING-IN-PUBLICATION DATA

Damon, Duane
    Mein Kampf: Hitler's blueprint for Aryan supremacy / by Duane Damon.
    p. cm. -- (Words that changed history)
Summary: Profiles the conditions that led to the rise of Adolf Hitler and his philosophy,
ultimately leading to Germany's defeat during World War II.
Includes bibliographical references and index.
ISBN 1-56006-800-0 (alk. paper)
1. Hitler, Adolf, 1889-1945. Mein Kampf.
2. Heads of state--Germany--Biography--Juvenile literature.
3. National socialism--History--Biography--Juvenile literature. [1. Hitler, Adolf, 1889-
1945. Mein Kampf. 2. Germany--History. 3. National socialism.] I. Title. II. Series.
    DD247.H5 D36 2003
    943.086'092--dc21

                                                                                    2002011028

Contents

Foreword

"We hold these truths to be self-evident, that all men are created equal, that they are endowed by their Creator with certain unalienable Rights, that among these are Life, Liberty and the pursuit of Happiness." So states one of America's most cherished documents, the Declaration of Independence. These words ripple through time. They represent the thoughts of the Declaration's author, Thomas Jefferson, but at the same time they reflect the attitudes of a nation in which individual rights were trampled by a foreign government. To many of Jefferson's contemporaries, these words characterized a revolutionary philosophy of liberty. Many Americans today still believe the ideas expressed in the Declaration were uniquely American. And while it is true that this document was a product of American ideals and values, its ideas did not spring from an intellectual vacuum. The Enlightenment, which had pervaded France and England for years, had proffered ideas of individual rights, and Enlightenment scholars drew their notions from historical antecedents tracing back to ancient Greece.

In essence, the Declaration was part of an ongoing historical dialogue concerning the conflict between individual rights and government powers. There is no doubt, however, that it made a palpable impact on its times. For colonists, the Declaration listed their grievances and set out the ideas for which they would stand and fight. These words changed history for Americans. But the Declaration also changed history for other nations; in France, revolutionaries would emulate concepts of self-rule to bring down their own monarchy and draft their own philosophies in a document known as the Declaration of the Rights of Man and of the Citizen. And the historical dialogue continues today in many third world nations.

Lucent Books's Words That Changed History series looks at oral and written documents in light of their historical context and their lasting impact. Some documents, such as the Declaration, spurred people to immediately change society; other documents fostered lasting intellectual debate. For example, Charles Darwin's treatise *On the Origin of Species* did not simply extend the discussion of human origins, it offered a theory of evolution which eventually would cause a schism between some religious and scientific thinkers. The debate still rages as people on both sides reaffirm their intellectual positions, even as new scientific evidence continues to impact the issue.

Students researching famous documents, the time periods in which they were prominent, or the issues they raise will find the books in this series both compelling and useful. Readers will see the chain of events that give rise to historical events. They will understand through the examination of specific documents that ideas or philosophies always have their antecedents, and they will learn how these documents carried on the legacy of influence by affecting people in other places or other times. The format for the series emphasizes these points by devoting chapters to the political or intellectual climate of the times, the values and prejudices of the drafters or speakers, the contents of the document and its impact on its contemporaries, and the manner in which perceptions of the document have changed through time.

In addition to their format, the books in Lucent's Words That Changed History series contain features that enhance understanding. Many primary and secondary source quotes give readers insight into the thoughts of the document's contemporaries as well as those who interpret the document's significance in hindsight. Sidebars interspersed throughout the text offer greater examination of relevant personages or significant events to provide readers with a broader historical context. Footnotes allow readers to verify the credibility of source material. Two bibliographies give students the opportunity to expand their research. And an appendix that includes excerpts as well as full text of original documents gives students access to the larger historical picture into which these documents fit.

History is often shaped by words. Oral and written documents concretize the thoughts of a select few, but they often transform the beliefs of an entire era or nation. As Confucius asserted, "Without knowing the force of words, it is impossible to know men." And understanding the power of words reveals a new way of understanding history.

A Primer for Hatred

It hardly looked like a prison cell at all. Cell Number 7 in Germany's Landsberg Prison was surprisingly large, with two big windows that admitted sunlight in generous amounts. Aside from the white iron bed and table there were bookcases stuffed with newspapers, magazines, and books. Gifts of fruit and wine arrived regularly. Bouquets of flowers from well-wishers splashed cheery colors against the drab walls. Perhaps most significantly, on a small table off to one side sat a borrowed typewriter.

The newly famous occupant of Cell Number 7 was formerly a soldier and recently a politician. He was not a physically impressive man. His smallish stature, sallow complexion, and quaint "toothbrush" mustache gave him more than a passing resemblance to the silent film comedian Charlie Chaplin. But here within the ancient walls of Landsberg Prison, thirty-five-year-old Adolf Hitler was grimly intent. As the months of 1924 passed, he was patiently biding his time and quietly scheming. And he was writing a book.

Into its pages Hitler poured his hatred, disgust, contempt, bigotry, and his lust for political and military control. This supposed life story and history of National Socialism, the movement Hitler led, would become nothing less than a primer for hatred. Its real "lessons" lay in gathering power, persecuting minorities, stealing territory, and mounting a second world conflict. Hitler was to follow the course he charted in his book to the peak of power and to the depths of mass murder and wholesale destruction.

Since the end of World War II, perplexing questions have troubled statesmen and students of history. More than half a century after its twelve-year reign of terror, historians still struggle to explain how the Third Reich of Adolf Hitler came to be. They continue to analyze the reasons the Nazi Party was so spectacularly and tragically successful. They still marvel at the way Hitler tapped into the fear, shame, and anger of the German nation and channeled those emotions so destructively.

Certainly, Germany had seen its share of great national leaders, from Frederick the Great to Otto von Bismarck. Yet none could approach the level of naked prejudice and hatred, the power of manipulating the masses, or the outright destructiveness of Hitler's Nazi regime. None left the German people so devastated, their cities and lands so ruined, their way of life so fully uprooted. And none had brought about such widespread carnage throughout Europe and other parts of the world. Not even the Great War of 1914–1918 had inflicted so much damage and human loss.

Perhaps there will never be any definitive answer to the puzzle of the Third Reich and its führer (leader). Even after decades of study, historians have found the man and his Nazi Party an enigma. "The more I learn about Adolf Hitler," biographer Alan Bullock has written, "the harder I find it to explain and accept what followed."[1] Still, many tantalizing hints and clues to this terrible mystery remain. Some of the most direct evidence has come to us from Hitler himself, contained in the pages of *Mein Kampf,* the book he wrote at the lowest point of his career. Part "autobiography," part racist ravings, part political scheming, it contains the sum of Hitler's hate-driven weltanschauung, or worldview. In this rambling—and often ranting—two-volume work, the future führer maps out with eerie accuracy the course he was charting for genocide and world domination. Ironically, at the time of its first publication, *Mein Kampf* attracted few buyers and fewer readers. Yet, as historian William L. Shirer suggests in *The Rise and Fall of the Third Reich,*

Had more non-Nazi Germans read it before 1933 and had the foreign statesmen of the world perused it carefully while there was still time, both Germany and the world might have been saved from catastrophe. For whatever other accusations can be made against Adolf Hitler, no one can accuse him of not putting down in writing exactly what kind of Germany he intended to make if he ever came to power.[2]

Adolf Hitler came tragically close to achieving the hate-driven goals he had outlined in *Mein Kampf.* Despite its eventual failure, his Third Reich succeeded in bringing about suffering and destruction on a level unparalleled in history. By the time Hitler at last fell victim to his own dark designs in 1945, the world had been changed forever.

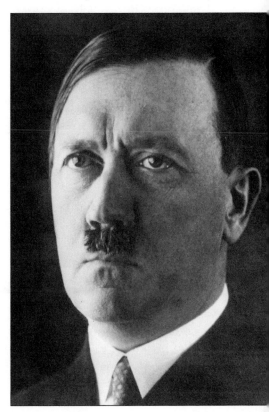

Adolf Hitler, architect of the Third Reich, based his ideology on hate and fear.

CHAPTER 1 A Proud Nation Humbled

The Third Reich of Adolf Hitler did not rise from some dark or evil void. The threads of its origins were woven into the very fabric of German life itself. Once a great and proud empire, Germany in the early twentieth century had been reduced by both war and peace to a fourth-rate power. Its territories had been plundered, its monarchy toppled, its national pride shattered. Germany was a nation in need of a savior. Adolf Hitler offered himself for that role. No matter how destructive his schemes, he could never have won the support of the German people if they had not first been willing to be inspired and led, and—very often—willing to look the other way.

To Germany in the 1920s and 1930s, Nazism was not a radically new phenomenon. In many ways it was merely a distorted extension of political movements that had come before. Hitler even named his regime the Third Reich in reference to its imperial predecessor, the late-nineteenth- and early-twentieth-century Second Reich.

The Second Reich

On the morning of March 9, 1888, Kaiser Wilhelm I, emperor of Germany, breathed his last in his palace bed in Berlin. Only two weeks shy of his ninety-first birthday, the old soldier had witnessed great changes during his lifetime. Most important had been the long-awaited formation of a unified Germany in 1871. For centuries, the kingdom had been little more than a sprawling collection of fiercely proud and quarrelsome states. But in that momentous year a new order had come to the region. A trio of European wars engineered by Wilhelm's chancellor Otto von Bismarck had paved the way for the historic union of those disparate territories. Dubbed "the Second Reich," the new empire seemed to promise all the glory of the First Reich of the Holy Roman Empire nine hundred years before. Unknown to the dying monarch, it would prove to be as short-lived as it was glorious.

Frederick III was already fifty-seven years old when he succeeded his father in March 1888. Ninety days later the new kaiser was dead of throat cancer. For the second time that year, the crown passed to another, and the fate of the German empire took a dramatic turn.

Germany and Her People

When Frederick's son took the throne in June, he took it by storm. Pompous, vain, deeply in love with all things royal and military, Wilhelm II conducted himself and his reign with generous servings of ceremony and splendor. Despite a withered left arm, the new kaiser cut a dashing figure as he attended military maneuvers and royal functions in full uniform. He thrilled his subjects with his ultimate plan for Germany, or *Weltpolitik:* to elevate the nation from a European entity to a world power. "We are destined to great things," Wilhelm declared, "and I am leading you to marvelous times."[3]

It was not hard for Germans of the era to be swept up in this kind of boast. Germany's 68 million people fell into roughly four social and economic classes. On the highest level was the aristocracy comprising rich and titled landowners and industrialists, higher-level educators, lawyers, and doctors. The upper middle class included landowners of medium wealth, owners of businesses, and high-ranking officials. Farmers, artisans, and tradespeople made up the lower middle class. Workers and peasants occupied the bottom rung of the scale. Two traits shared by all the classes were a love of royal pomp and grandeur, and a dream of better things ahead. Wilhelm symbolized all these things to his subjects, and in return they gave him their trust. In the bargain, however, came the loss of certain personal freedoms. Historian and photojournalist Stefan Lorant, born in 1901, was a firsthand observer of German society:

Kaiser Wilhelm II (front, left), fond of military regalia, observes military maneuvers in full uniform.

Records of every person were meticulously kept, with full details about his occupation, wealth and social standing. Every change in the citizen's status was dutifully noted by the mushrooming bureaucracy. If someone moved to a new residence, the police had to be notified and a card filed; if someone hired a servant girl, she had to be registered on a yellow form.[4]

In keeping with this policy of control, military service was mandatory for every German male. During his hitch in one of the armed forces, a young man was taught obedience above all. He learned to live simply and to work hard. "In those years," Stefan Lorant points out, "his individuality was weakened, his initiative deadened, and he acquired a lifelong habit of dependence upon authority."[5]

Despite its regimented society—or perhaps partly because of it—Germany was growing into an industrial giant. As factories sprang up in urban areas, farmers and peasants left farms and homesteads and moved to the cities. Here they joined other city dwellers to labor eleven or more hours a day, six days a week. The result was a steady rise in the nation's industrial output. By 1900 Germany was outproducing France and Great Britain. By 1914 only the industries of the United States turned out a greater volume of goods.

The Great War

Yet all was not well with the land of the kaisers and Germany's neighbors. Geography and history were continually drawing the nations of Europe into conflict. Physically surrounded by other Old World powers, Germany was often in the thick of political feuds and squabbles. Centuries of wars, broken treaties, and shifting alliances had taken their toll.

Wilhelm II's neighbors were only too aware of his dream of world domination. Immediately to the west, the French, longtime antagonists of Germany, worried that they might be the first target of the kaiser's scheme. Moreover, France had lost the border region of Alsace-Lorraine to the Germans in the war of 1871, and was determined to get it back. Across the English Channel, Great Britain was jealously protective of two things: British supremacy at sea, and Britain's prominent position in world trade. The British saw Germany as a menacing threat to both. Austria-Hungary, meanwhile, feared German aggression would threaten its own hold on the states of Czechoslovakia, Serbia, Bosnia, and Croatia. Across the face of Europe, tensions were high and political alliances complex.

Hitler and the Great War

World War I brought a strange kind of salvation to Adolf Hitler. Freed from his bleak existence of drifting and failure, he wrangled a place in the Sixteenth Bavarian Reserve Infantry Regiment as a dispatch runner. While not actually frontline battle, it was nonetheless dangerous work and he took to it. Twice he won the Iron Cross medal for valor.

Here in a letter to a Munich acquaintance, quoted by historian E.J. Feuchtwanger in From Weimar to Hitler, *the young Hitler describes advancing with his unit under British and Belgian bombardment near Ypres, Belgium.*

"Now the first shrapnel hisses over us and explodes at the edge of the forest, splintering trees as if they were straws. . . . We crawl on our stomachs to the edge of the forest. Above us are howls and hisses, splintered branches and trees surround us. Then again shells explode at the edge of the forest and hurl clouds of stones, earth and sand into the air, tear the heaviest trees out by their roots, and choke everything in a yellow-green, terribly stinking steam. . . . Four times we advance and have to go back; from my whole batch [of fellow dispatch runners] only one remains, beside me, finally he also falls. A shot tears off my right coat sleeve, but like a miracle I remain safe and alive."

Yet when among his comrades off the battlefield, he often took his patriotism to extremes. In a foreshadowing of his future days, Hitler's passion for his beliefs drew the notice—not always favorable—of those around him. In Adolf Hitler, *John Toland relates the reactions of many of his fellow soldiers.*

"'We all cursed him and found him intolerable,' one of the men in his company later recalled. 'There was this white crow among us that didn't go along with us when we damned the war to hell.' Another man described him as sitting 'in the corner of our mess [eating area] holding his head between his hands, in deep contemplation. Suddenly he would leap up and, running about excitedly, say that in spite of our big guns victory would be denied us, for the invisible foes of the German people were a greater danger than the biggest cannon of the enemy.' Whereupon he would launch into a vitriolic attack on these 'invisible foes'—the Jews and the Marxists. Had he not learned in Vienna that they were the source of all evil?"

Then, on June 28, 1914, Archduke Franz Ferdinand of Austria-Hungary was assassinated in Bosnia by Serbian nationalists. Enraged by the murder of the heir to the throne, Austria-Hungary declared war on Serbia one month later. Russia quickly lined up behind Serbia. In support, France and Great Britain declared war on Germany. Allying himself with Austria-Hungary, Kaiser Wilhelm declared war on France, Great Britain, and Russia. "The lamps are going out all over Europe," said British diplomat Sir Edward Grey. "We shall not see them lit again in our lifetime."[6]

The conflict that followed was like none the world had ever seen. Within weeks, all Europe was transformed into a war zone. For three years, German, Austrian, French, British, Russian, Polish, and Italian armies battled one another at places ever after associated with carnage—the Ardennes, Verdun, the Marne. In the spring of 1917 the United States entered the conflict for its final eighteen months. Autumn of the following year saw the surrender of Germany's allies, followed by demands for an armistice by the German High Command. That armistice was signed on November 11 in a railroad car in Compiègne, France.

The Hated Treaty

The losses suffered during the war by the nations of Europe were of a magnitude never before witnessed in history. In all, nearly 10 million men had died, 20 million had suffered wounds, and some 6 million were reported missing. Destruction to cities, farms, and property was nearly incalculable. Germany, many had decided, was the cause of it all. Therefore, Germany must pay. So believed most of the delegates who gathered in Paris early in 1919 to formulate the final peace treaty. Great Britain, France, Italy, and the United States headed the conference; Germany was not even permitted to participate in drafting the Treaty of Versailles.

Under its terms, Germany was held responsible for all damages to lives and property incurred in the war. Germany was stripped of most of the territory it had taken during the recent war and earlier ones as well. In addition, the treaty reduced the army of the defeated nation to one hundred thousand men, the navy to fifteen thousand. The German armed forces were allowed no more than twenty-four ships, with no submarines or military aircraft. "Germany," summarized British historian E.J. Feuchtwanger, "was effectively barred for the foreseeable future from becoming a world power again in a military sense."[7]

The financial punishment was even more severe. The treaty called for an initial payment of 5 billion dollars in gold marks to be paid within two years. Further payments could be made in goods and resources—coal, cattle, lumber, ships, trains, and other commodities.

At the insistence of U.S. president Woodrow Wilson, a new provision was added to the treaty. It called for a League of Nations, an international assembly designed to discuss ideas and resolve international disputes. Ironically, the U.S. Congress would later reject membership in the league. Skeptical of Europe's ability to remain at peace, Americans were in no mood to become further entangled in the problems of foreign nations. America's absence from the League of Nations would be a serious roadblock to the world security Wilson had so desperately sought.

The New Republic

The completed peace treaty was presented to the Germans for ratification in the spring of 1919. Yet Wilhelm II, who had done so much to start the war, had fled to Holland the day before the November armistice. Communists and other radical elements took advantage of the moment to stage uprisings and riots in Berlin, Munich, and other cities.

Meanwhile, a democratic republic was replacing the monarchy. Convening in the town of Weimar in February 1919, the national assembly drafted a liberal constitution giving its citizens broad personal

Allied officers stand on tables and chairs to get every possible glimpse of an historic event, the signing of the Treaty of Versailles in 1919, officially holding Germany responsible for World War I.

freedoms, including voting rights for women. Friedrich Ebert, a Social Democrat, was elected provisional president. To the hapless Ebert and his colleagues in the Reichstag, the German parliament, fell the thankless job of voting the Versailles treaty up or down.

It was political suicide either way. The German people, proud of their Teutonic heritage as a race of warriors, had entered the war confident of victory. Kept in the dark by military leaders about the war's progress, they had taken its outcome for granted. They even assumed the Versailles treaty would let Germany off lightly. Then came the harsh reality of its terms. "They came as a staggering blow to a people who had insisted on deluding themselves to the last moment," wrote American journalist William L. Shirer. "Angry mass meetings were organized throughout the country to protest against the treaty and to demand that Germany refuse to sign it."[8] On the other hand, rejecting the treaty would likely mean the total destruction of the German army by the Allies.

Despite the storm of opposition, leaders of the new republic had little choice. Encouraged by German army officials, the Reichstag voted for approval. The final signing of the treaty took place in the Hall of Mirrors at Versailles on June 28, 1919. With the stroke of a pen, Germany's humiliation was complete.

Stabbed in the Back?

Now the humbled nation was left to deal with the bitter fruits of defeat. German soldiers returning home discovered a country in the throes of political and economic turmoil. They found jobs to be few, food scarce, and inflation rampant. The German mark had shrunk to one-fifth of its prewar value. Facing starvation, many Germans were reduced to selling personal and family belongings for a pittance.

To a once-proud people, this humiliation was galling. Then, as if to stoke the fires of resentment further, a story surfaced that Field Marshal Paul von Hindenburg had told the national assembly of a conversation he had had with a British general. The German army had not really lost the war, the Englishman had said. The politicians who had agreed to the November armistice had betrayed the army and the German people. They had, in effect, "stabbed Germany in the back."

True or not, Hindenburg's tale struck a nerve with citizens across the country. It inflamed the wounded pride of Germans in a way that would have consequences for years to come. As Stefan Lorant explained:

> No German wanted to believe in defeat. The people could not comprehend that all their sacrifices had been in vain. They

In impoverished post–WWI Germany, hungry children at a street kitchen wait eagerly for servings of warm soup.

looked for a scapegoat—and soon found one: the "November criminals." It was the new Republican government that had sold them out, that was responsible for the defeat—not the kaiser and his generals. And the people believed the blatant lie.[9]

Believing that lie made it a little easier for the German people to cope with their feelings of failure, betrayal, and loss. At the same time, it made them still more vulnerable to the tantalizing message of Adolf Hitler. Like them, Hitler had been raised on Wilhelm's grandiose promises and had experienced World War I and its subsequent humiliation firsthand. He possessed an uncanny instinct for telling people what they wanted to hear. At this pivotal moment he appeared on the scene; many Germans found it all too easy to follow the man who, two decades later, would lead them into still lower depths of shame and defeat. His background, however, did not seem to indicate either greatness or infamy.

Birth of a Dictator

"Today it seems to me providential that Fate should have chosen Braunau on the Inn as my birthplace." Thus the opening line of Adolf Hitler's autobiography, *Mein Kampf*, speaks warmly of the burg in Austria where he was born thirteen months after the death of Kaiser Wilhelm I. Yet "this little town on the Inn, gilded by the rays of German martyrdom"[10] was the scene of a less than idyllic childhood.

The Legacy of Versailles

The treaty that made the peace inflicted further suffering on the German people. At the center of the peace
treaty was Article 231, the so-called War
Guilt Clause. Its wording left little doubt as to the
Allies' intentions:

"The Allied and Associated Governments declare, and Germany acknowledges, that Germany and her allies are as perpe-
trators responsible for all the losses and damages suffered by the
Allied and Associated Governments and their citizens, as a result of
the war forced upon them by the attack of Germany and her allies."

*"The main purpose of this article," writes historian E.J. Feuchtwanger
in* From Weimar to Hitler, *"was to pin on Germany the responsibility
for reparations and to provide a moral justification for this responsibility." The idea that Germany should pay for war damages over-
shadowed the Versailles conference. France demanded aid in restoring
its vital and heavily damaged northern provinces. England suffered
less physical damage but staggering financial losses from the war. And
the United States had given billions of dollars in war loans to the Allies, loans she could ill afford to let go unpaid.*

*For the Germans, the picture was even worse. Not only was Ger-
many internationally in debt for war damages, but she was stripped of
nearly 15 percent of her territory. The defeated nation was forced to
suffer huge losses in land, money, and most importantly, face. The Allied delegations called the Treaty of Versailles a victory for the forces
of right. To the German people, it smelled like revenge.*

In Mein Kampf, *Adolf Hitler made this prediction for revenge of
his own:*

"How each one of the points of that Treaty could be branded in the
minds and hearts of the German people until sixty million men and
women find their souls aflame with a feeling of rage and shame; and
a torrent of fire bursts forth as from a furnace . . . with the common
cry: 'We will have arms again!'"

His father, Alois Hitler Sr., was an Austrian civil servant assigned to
the town as inspector of customs. He was a proud and formidable man
who meted out severe whippings to his children, most often Adolf and
his older half-brother Alois Jr. Alois's second wife, the passive and sen-
sitive Klara Pölzl Hitler, gave birth to Adolf on April 20, 1889. He was
her fourth child, the first to live beyond a few years. The deaths of her

first three children probably deepened Klara's need to pamper and spoil Adolf, at least until his younger sister, Paula, arrived.

Early Youth

Adolf grew into a stubborn child who attracted few friends. In school he seldom felt challenged or even interested. Despite his general indifference to the classroom, Adolf developed an early passion for reading. In *Mein Kampf* he recounted how, at the age of ten or eleven, his bookish tendencies led him to an important discovery.

> Rummaging through my father's library, I had come across various books of a military nature, among them a popular edition of the Franco-German War of 1870–71. It consisted of two issues of an illustrated periodical from those years, which now became my favorite reading matter. It was not long before the great heroic struggle had become my greatest inner experience. From then on I became more and more enthusiastic about everything that was in any way connected with war or, for that matter, with soldiering.[11]

Adolf Hitler's father, Alois Hitler Sr. (pictured), was a stern man who often beat his children.

Adolf soon acquired another interest: art. Not surprisingly, the chief subjects of his nearly constant sketching were military figures, especially the great Teutonic heroes of German mythology. But while Adolf nursed his artistic ambitions, Alois Sr. decreed that his son would follow in his footsteps. Equally stubborn, the younger Hitler refused.

With the death of Alois Sr. in early 1903, the thirteen-year-old Adolf was now free to pursue anything he wished, which, as it turned out, was very little. Within two years he dropped out of school, still living with his mother but resisting steady work. August Kubizek, his only friend during this time, later penned this portrait of Adolf:

> He sketched, he painted, he wrote poems and he read. I cannot remember that Adolf was ever idle or felt bored even for a single hour. . . . [But] there was no apparent purpose, no clear goal. He only accumulated with unbounded energy impressions, experience and material. What would ever become of it all remained an open question. He did nothing but search.[12]

Dreams of a Wanderer

During this period Adolf developed two more passions. One was architecture; the other, opera. He was aroused and enchanted by the tales of heroes and heroines portrayed in the stirring works of the German composer Richard Wagner. "My youthful enthusiasm for the master of Bayreuth [Wagner's home city and the site of an annual opera festival] knew no bounds," Hitler recalled in *Mein Kampf.* "Again and again I was drawn to his works."[13]

Two years after dropping out of school, Adolf moved to the Austrian capital of Vienna and applied to the Academy of Fine Arts. He managed to pass the first part of the entrance examination, but failed the second.

Ten-year-old Adolf Hitler (top row, center) poses with his school classmates. Although fond of reading, the boy was an indifferent student.

"In That Hour It Began"

The youthful Hitler's period in Linz was brightened by his friendship with August Kubizek, a schoolmate whose interest in music nearly matched Adolf's passion for art and architecture. In this passage from his book, The Young Hitler I Knew, *Kubizek tells of attending a performance of* Rienzi, *a Wagner opera, with his friend. The story of the rise of the young Rienzi to be the tribune of ancient Rome had a profound effect on Adolf. "Usually, after an artistic experience that had moved him, he would start talking right away, sharply criticizing the performance," August wrote. "But after* Rienzi *he remained quiet a long while."*

"As if propelled by an invisible force, Adolf climbed to the top of the Freinberg [a hill outside Linz]. . . . [He] stood in front of me; and now he gripped both my hands and held them tight. He had never made such a gesture before. I felt from the grasp of his hands how deeply moved he was. His eyes were feverish with excitement. . . .

Never before and never again have I heard Adolf Hitler speak as he did in that hour, as we stood there alone under the stars. . . . It was as if another being spoke out of his body, and moved him as much as it did me. . . . I will not attempt to interpret this phenomenon, but it was a state of complete ecstasy and rapture, in which he transferred the character of Rienzi without even mentioning him as a model or example, with visionary power to the plane of his own ambitions. . . . He conjured up in grandiose, inspiring pictures his own future and that of his people.

Hitherto I had been convinced that my friend wanted to become an artist, a painter, or perhaps an architect. . . . But now he was talking of a *mandate* which, one day, he would receive from the people, to lead them out of servitude to the heights of freedom. . . . It was an unknown youth who spoke to me in that strange hour. He spoke of a special mission which would one day be entrusted to him, and I, his only listener, could hardly understand what he meant. Many years had to pass before I realized the significance of this enraptured hour for my friend."

In 1939, at the height of his power as Nazi dictator of Germany, Hitler was visited by his boyhood friend who reminded the Führer of that fateful evening on the hill.

"He was visibly pleased that my account confirmed his own recollections. I was also present when Adolf Hitler retold this sequel to the performance of *Rienzi* in Linz to Frau Wagner [widow of the opera's composer], at whose home we were both guests. . . . The words with which Hitler concluded his story to Frau Wagner are also unforgettable to me. He said solemnly, 'In that hour it began.'"

He was still reeling from this setback when he learned his mother was dying. Following her death on December 21, 1907, the grief-stricken young man again applied to the academy. This time, he failed even to pass the first part of the exam. A stunned Adolf now took stock. He was eighteen years old, without a high school education, unable to study art or architecture, and jobless. "The fulfillment of my artistic dream," he admitted in *Mein Kampf*, "seemed physically impossible."[14]

Hitler was deeply affected by the death of his devoted mother, Klara (pictured), in 1907.

Dark Days in Vienna

Depressed by his failures, Adolf began to slide backward. He tried selling his drawings and paintings to Vienna's art vendors, but met with only limited success. As his money ran low, he moved to cheaper lodgings; when it ran out, he moved to the streets. For months he lived in a dingy hostel for homeless men. Of this time Hitler wrote, "Hunger was then my faithful bodyguard; he never left me for a moment and partook of all I had."[15]

Meanwhile, on the streets of Vienna, the vagrant artist was undergoing a grim self-education. He gives an example in *Mein Kampf:*

> Once, as I was strolling through the Inner City, I suddenly encountered an apparition in a black caftan and black hair locks. Is this a Jew? was my first thought.

> For, to be sure, they had not looked like that in Linz. I observed the man furtively and cautiously, but the longer I stared at this foreign face, scrutinizing feature for feature, the more my first question assumed a new form.

> Is this a German?[16]

At this point Hitler had not fully developed his racist and nationalist beliefs. But dark theories were already beginning to form. "In this
period there took shape within me a world picture and a philosophy
which became the granite foundation of all my acts," he wrote later.
"In addition to what I then created, I have had to learn little; and I
have had to alter nothing."[17]

This was essentially true. Hitler's fundamental political and social
ideas were formed during his teen and young adult years. Unfortunately for Germany and the world, it was "a world picture and a philosophy" based on the observations and assumptions of a self-absorbed,
unhappy, and self-deluding individual. Never able to accept personal
responsibility for his problems or decisions, Hitler found it only too
easy to transfer the blame for misfortune or misery onto other individuals. If he did poorly in school, it was because his teachers were
"abnormal" or "slightly mad."[18] His failure to make a career in art was
due to "the fact that trade in works of art was in Jewish hands."[19] Ir-
responsible and twisted, it was a pattern of thinking he would follow
until his death.

Deliverance: The Great War

For the young Hitler, now living in Munich, the outbreak of World
War I in June 1914 was a godsend. "Overpowered by stormy enthusiasm," he recalled in *Mein Kampf*, "I fell down on my knees and
thanked Heaven from an over-flowing heart for granting me the good
fortune of being permitted to live at this time."[20] By petitioning the
king of Bavaria, Adolf landed a spot in a Bavarian infantry regiment.
Despite being described as "an odd character"[21] by one comrade in
arms, Adolf was happy in his role as a soldier. "At the age of twenty-
five," writes Hitler biographer Ian Kershaw, "it gave him for the first
time in his life a cause, a commitment, comradeship, an external dis-
cipline, a sort of regular employment, a sense of well-being, and—
more than that—a sense of belonging."[22]

For four years he served with bravery and distinction. Then, on
October 13, 1918, his regiment was hit by a British barrage of mus-
tard gas. Days later Adolf found himself in a military hospital in
Pasewalk, temporarily blind. While he recuperated, startling news
arrived: the German army in France had surrendered to the Allies.
Adolf was sick with shock. "Everything went black before my eyes,"
he reported in *Mein Kampf*. "I tottered and groped my way back to
the dormitory, threw myself on my bunk, and dug my burning head
into my blanket and pillow."[23]

The conflict that rescued Hitler from a life of aimless obscurity had
ended in defeat, shame, and disillusionment for Germany and the

Hitler (top, second from right) poses with other recuperating soldiers at a military hospital in 1918. While there, Hitler learned that Germany had lost the war.

Central Powers. Unfortunately, the mind-numbing loss of life, land, and national pride would later play directly into the Austrian's hands. "The war," biographer Alan Bullock points out, "and the impact of war upon the individual lives of millions of Germans, were among the essential conditions for the rise of Hitler and the Nazi Party."[24]

And Now, Politics

Adolf Hitler and his fellow soldiers came home to a different Germany. Led by the struggling Weimar government, the nation's political structure was fragmented and confused. Dozens of fledgling parties competed for public attention. But social unrest was not limited to Germany; in 1919 Communist supporters rose up and overthrew the Moscow government in Russia. And now bolshevism (Russian communism) was beginning to find favor with Germans disillusioned by the war and the failings of the Weimar Republic.

The defeated German army had reformed into a reduced force called the Reichswehr. Its concerns were twofold. On one side, the military, still led by conservative elites such as the aristocratic Junkers of Prussia, distrusted the democratic policies of the new republic; on the other, it feared the possibility of a Communist takeover. Part of the Reichswehr's mission was to keep tabs on potentially subversive groups on both the right and left extremes. In September 1919 the recently recovered Corporal Hitler was dispatched to monitor a tiny group of workers called the Deutsche Arbeiterpartei (DAP), or German Workers' Party.

At one gathering in a Munich beer hall, Hitler was unimpressed by the speeches he heard. Rising to leave, he was halted by the words of the next speaker. This man declared his belief that Bavaria should split off from the main part of Germany and join with Austria as a South German nation. Aroused to fury, Hitler fired back a rebuttal so stinging that the speaker meekly left the building. The group's leader was so taken by the stranger's fire that he pressed a party pamphlet on him before he, too, disappeared. As he left, Hitler had no inkling that he had just taken part in a meeting of the future Nazi Party.

Early the next morning, a sleepless Hitler took a look at the pamphlet he had been given. To his surprise, its author expressed views strikingly similar to Hitler's own. The recent war, the pamphlet read, had been given away by the "November criminals" and Jewish and Communist elements; to reclaim its former glory, Germany must regain all its former territories and replace the shaky republic with a strong nationalist government. When he received an invitation soon afterward to join the DAP, Hitler hesitated, but only briefly. As he wrote in *Mein Kampf:*

> I had long been resolved to engage in political activity; that this could be done only in a new movement was likewise clear to me. . . . This absurd little organization with its few members seemed to me to posses the one advantage that it had not

German officers interview volunteers for the highly politicized Reichswehr, the *Weimar-era army.*

frozen into an "organization," but left the individual an opportunity for real personal activity. . . . After two days of agonized pondering and reflection, I finally came to the conviction that I had to take this step. It was the most decisive resolve of my life. From here there was and could be no turning back.[25]

"I Could Speak!"

In the days that followed, Hitler threw himself into party activities with a remarkable zeal and drive. Impatient with the group's pitiful size, Hitler pushed for larger meetings. Placing a notice in a Munich newspaper brought in over one hundred people for the very next gathering. For the first time, Hitler himself took the podium. "I spoke for thirty minutes," Hitler recorded in *Mein Kampf,* "and what before I had simply felt within me, without in any way knowing it, was now proved by reality: I could speak!"[26] With his entrancing eyes, dramatic gestures, and penetrating voice, Hitler quickly became the most popular speaker in the DAP, then in all Munich.

In speech after speech, Hitler pounded home his bold ideas for the DAP program. They included a call for the unification of all Germans in a Greater Germany, and refashioning the state into a strong central power. Going a step further, the Austrian trumpeted the concept of lebensraum (living space) as devised by DAP member, and later Nazi Party philosopher, Alfred Rosenberg. Under this theory a nation required sufficient space to remain strong. The "pure" blood of the Aryan race—ancient ancestors of the German people—entitled it to the lands of weaker nations in order to reach its potential greatness. Hitler ended by condemning the Treaty of Versailles and advocating the barring of Jews from public office or German citizenship. Thundering applause greeted his speech. The DAP's first mass rally had proved a stunning success. "By it, the party burst the narrow bonds of a small club," Hitler later exulted, "and for the first time exerted a determining influence on the mightiest factor of our time, public opinion."[27]

"On the Political Map"

The greater Hitler's influence within the DAP, the greater his need to control, protect, and promote it. With the help of Ernst Röhm, a Munich army captain, Hitler established the Sturmabteilung (Storm Detachment), known as the SA, which Röhm commanded. Little more than organized gangs of street thugs, thousands of these "Brownshirts"—so called for the color of their uniforms—stood ready to attack Hitler's political opponents by disrupting their meetings, often violently.

Four "Brownshirts," Nazi Party storm troopers who were little more than street thugs, give the Nazi salute.

Next, Hitler changed the party's name to Nationalsozialistische Deutsche Arbeiterpartei, or the National Socialist German Workers' Party. The new title, he felt, would more clearly identify the party as a recognizable organization with distinct policies. The shortened form of the title's first word became the name destined to reshape history: Nazi. Then, believing "the party comrades lacked any outward sign of their common bond,"[28] Hitler himself selected a symbol for the movement. It was the ancient Hakenkreuz (crooked cross), or swastika. Set in black inside a white disk against a field of red, the new party insignia soon appeared on Nazi flags, armbands, and banners across Munich.

Despite these changes, the party's appeal remained limited. "Hitler's speeches put him on the political map in Munich," writes historian Ian Kershaw. "But he was still very much a local."[29] By the fall of 1923 Hitler had his fill of obscurity. Now the virtual head of the Nazi Party, the restless Führer (leader) was ready to break out onto the national scene. A scheme began to form in Hitler's mind, one that was daring and dangerous. In attempting it, Nazis were to risk everything in one desperate gamble—an ill-conceived venture that was fated to fail.

The Nazi Bible:
Mein Kampf

Throughout his dark career, Adolf Hitler displayed a remarkable ability to survive political defeat and reemerge, his power intact and even enhanced. In the next two years, Hitler would risk everything he had achieved, fall into obscurity and disgrace, and rise again to the peak of power in Germany. At his low point, he wrote the book that mapped out the route he intended to take to world domination.

All through the early 1920s, circumstances worked in Hitler's favor. As if to encourage his national ambitions, conditions in Germany were only growing worse. The economy was in crisis. While the value of the German mark plummeted to a near worthless 4 billion marks to the dollar, the people sank deeper into poverty and help-lessness. "All they knew," wrote William L. Shirer, "was that a large bank account could not buy a straggly bunch of carrots, a half peck of potatoes, a few ounces of sugar, a pound of flour . . . and they knew hunger when it gnawed at them, as it did daily."[30] Since the Republic had failed to fend off this disaster, Hitler rationalized, the Republic must be brought down.

The Beer Hall Putsch

Oddly enough, Hitler says little in *Mein Kampf* about his attempt to overthrow the Berlin government. Whether it remained a painful memory or he simply thought it unwise to remind the public of the debacle is not clear. In any case, word of a political meeting of un-usual importance reached Hitler early in November 1923. Attending this gathering would be the three top leaders of Bavaria, the southern German region where Munich was located. State Commissioner Gustav von Kahr was to be joined by General Otto von Lossow, com-mander of the Bavarian Reichswehr, or regular army, and Colonel Hans von Seisser, head of the state police. Together they were sched-uled to address three thousand patrons of a huge beer hall called the Bürgerbräukeller on November 8. For Hitler's scheme the time, place, and circumstances seemed ideal.

On the appointed evening, Commissioner Kahr was addressing the crowded hall when a contingent of SA troops surrounded the build-ing. Nazi members Rudolf Hess and Hermann Göring—both World War I fighter pilots—and Hitler bodyguard Ulrich Graf led the storm troopers into the main room. Already inside patiently sipping a beer was Hitler himself. He pulled his revolver, climbed atop a table, and fired into the air.

"The National Revolution has begun!" he shouted. "This building is occupied by six hundred armed men. No one may leave the hall."[31] Next he ordered Kahr, Lossow, and Seisser into a side room for a private conversation. If they would join the putsch, Hitler promised, he would award them key posts in the new Reich he was establishing with General Erich von Ludendorff. Ludendorff was among the greatest heroes of the recent war, and his name carried substantial weight. In spite of this bait, Kahr, Lossow, and Seisser stubbornly refused to answer.

Frustrated, Hitler resorted to bluff. He returned to the main hall and announced that the three leaders agreed to join him in the new national government to be led by himself. He and General Ludendorff, he declared, were ready to march on Berlin and overthrow the government. Hitler next brought out Kahr, Lossow, Seisser, and the newly arrived Ludendorff to pledge their loyalty to the new regime. Then Hitler left the beer hall to personally take charge of a skirmish between army troops and Nazi sympathizers across town. It was a mistake. On his return a few hours later, a stunned Hitler found the prisoners gone and his revolution in jeopardy.

Trying to salvage the botched Beer Hall Putsch, a smiling Rudolf Hess (center) and other SA troops assembled in Munich on November 8th for a march on the city government.

On the Firing Line

Ludendorff now put forward an ambitious plan of his own: march on the center of Munich and seize control of government offices. Hitler hesitated. Without the support of either the police or the army, the overthrow of the government now promised to be a drawn-out, bloody business. Yet, reluctantly, he agreed.

Eleven o'clock the next morning found Hitler, Ludendorff, and a column of three thousand SA troops marching toward the center of the city. Striding along beside them were Göring, Graf, Alfred Rosenberg, and Max von Scheubner-Richter, a Hitler aide. Their destination: the building that housed the War Ministry. Here Ernst Röhm and a Nazi unit were surrounded by soldiers of the Reichswehr. When Hitler and his forces attempted to enter a plaza leading to the ministry, a crew of one hundred policemen barred their way.

Then a shot sounded. In reply a volley of pistol and rifle shot echoed across the plaza. Göring fell to the pavement with a thigh wound. Mortally hit, Scheubner-Richter also dropped. Hitler, who had linked arms with Scheubner-Richter, was jerked downward. He struck the ground hard, dislocating his shoulder. Ludendorff, meanwhile, walked fearlessly—and alone—through the police line toward the plaza, where he was arrested.

Leaving Scheubner-Richter dead and Göring wounded, Hitler let himself be hustled into a waiting car. He was driven to temporary safety at the country home of his friend Ernst Hanfstängl, where he was nursed by Hanfstängl's wife. Two days later he was arrested, as Röhm and other Nazis had been.

General Ludendorff's proposal to seize government offices in Munich was supported by three thousand Nazi soldiers, including this group of storm troopers.

In all, sixteen Nazi followers and three policemen had been killed. The Berlin government responded to the attempted coup by officially banning the Nazi Party. While Hitler and his cronies awaited trial, they had time to reflect on their failure. "The Nazi putsch had ended in fiasco," wrote William L. Shirer. "The party was dissolved. National Socialism, to all appearances, was dead. Its dictatorial leader, who had run away at the first hail of bullets, seemed utterly discredited, his meteoric political career at an end."[32]

Victory in Defeat

Not surprisingly, the first reaction of Adolf Hitler to his indictment for treason was one of depression and defeat. Ian Kershaw described those days in his biography of the Nazi leader:

> He had initially refused to say anything, and announced that he was going on a hunger strike. At this time, he plainly saw everything as lost. According to the prison psychologist—though speaking many years after the event—Hitler stated: "I've had enough. I'm finished. If I had a revolver, I would take it."[33]

But the Austrian was nothing if not resilient. When his trial opened on February 24, it was a different Hitler who sat in the prisoner's dock. Gone was his sense of failure and loss. In its place was the grim resolve of one who had no intentions of accepting defeat. In the outside world, meanwhile, another change had taken place. Hitler's thwarted putsch had thrust his name into every newspaper in Europe and elsewhere. Defeat had accomplished what speeches and rallies had so far failed to do: It had brought Adolf Hitler worldwide notoriety.

The celebrated prisoner lost little time in turning his trial for treason into his own personal pulpit. Instead of trying to play down his role in the attempted takeover, Hitler boasted of it. "I alone bear responsibility," he told the court. "But I am not a criminal because of that. If today I stand here as a revolutionary, it is as a revolutionary against the revolution. There is no such thing as high treason against the traitors of 1918."[34]

He easily dominated the courtroom, shouting questions and accusations at the prosecution and its witnesses. "You may pronounce us guilty a thousand times over," he told the court in his final speech. "But the goddess of the eternal court of history will smile and tear to tatters the brief [arguments] of the state prosecutor and the sentence of this court. For she acquits us."[35]

The prisoner's prediction was not far off the mark. General Ludendorff was set free; Hitler, as expected, was found guilty of treason. Yet his sentence was surprisingly light—five years imprisonment with

Hitler (in raincoat) and Ludendorff (left of Hitler) pose with other defendants during their Munich trial for treason.

parole possible in six months. Disgusted by what he had witnessed, one German journalist derided the trial as "a Munich political carnival."[36] But the Nazi chief had reason to be satisfied. More than anything else, his trial for high treason had been an all-out propaganda battle, and Hitler had won it.

Hitler At Bay

Life for Landsberg Prison's most famous inmate was hardly an ordeal. His cell was spacious and the view from his windows cheery. Hitler ate well and enjoyed friendly and even respectful treatment from the warden and guards. He was permitted to receive gifts and visitors. Several of his fellow putschists were also jailed at Landsberg, providing Hitler with a sympathetic and literally captive audience. Yet as the first half of 1924 slipped past, his attention turned to something new. On July 7 the German newspaper *Der Völkischer Kurier* reported that Hitler had "requested his adherents not to visit him in prison since he had so much work and was also engaged in writing a book."[37]

"Without my imprisonment," Hitler later acknowledged, "*Mein Kampf* would never have been written. That period gave me the chance of deepening the various notions for which I then had only an instinctive feeling."[38] Privately, the prisoner had been consulting with Max Amann, formerly Hitler's sergeant in the Bavarian army and now head of the Nazi publishing house, Franz Eher Verlag. To Amann, Hitler proposed a book based on his own experiences that would chronicle the events leading up to the Beer Hall Putsch. To be titled

Four and a Half Years of Struggle Against Lies, Stupidity, and Cowardice, it was to conclude with a stirring account of the putsch's collapse. Amann was convinced that such a book would have strong appeal. After all, had Hitler's performance at his recent trial not drawn a substantial number of Germans over to the National Socialist school of thought? And had those same citizens not cast votes in the recent election, increasing Nazi strength in the Reichstag?

But Hitler was thinking on a broader scale. With its leader imprisoned, internal dissent was fragmenting the Nazi Party. Members had taken to wrangling over party principles and goals; some dared to criticize their Führer as a prima donna who had gotten out of control. What his splintered party needed, Hitler believed, was more than a mere history of the Nazi movement. "I decided to set forth, in two volumes, the aims of our movement," he stated in the book's preface, "and also to draw a picture of its development."[39] In addition, its author hoped, it would help reestablish his position as Nazi Party leader.

Journalist and biographer Joachim C. Fest believes Hitler harbored a more subtle motive for writing *Mein Kampf:* "Here was his chance to prove that despite his lack of schooling, despite his failure to be admitted to the Academy, despite his humiliating past in the home for men, he had reached the lofty heights of bourgeois culture."[40] In short, Hitler held in his hands the chance to reinvent himself as the tragic, yet ultimately heroic figure destined to lead his nation to its greatest glory.

A reflective Hitler peers from a window at Landsberg Prison. He spent long hours here dictating Mein Kampf *to followers.*

The Birth of the Nazi "Bible"

A determined Hitler now set to work. Too undisciplined a writer to spend endless hours bent over a table, pen in hand, the Führer dictated the text to others. The first was his own chauffeur Emil Maurice, who daily pecked away on a typewriter lent to Hitler by the prison warden. Then Rudolf Hess arrived at Landsberg. The

Backdrop for a Book: Landsberg Prison

Foreshadowing the title of his book, Adolf Hitler penned these words in his diary shortly after his conviction for treason: "The trial of common narrow-mindedness and personal spite is over—and today starts My Struggle, Landsberg on 1 April 1924." For the next eight months, the ancient walls of the prison fortress at Landsberg am Lech, Germany, were to mark the limits of his existence.

Located some forty miles west of Munich, the town of Landsberg snuggled comfortably in the Lech River valley. Wooded heights stretched steeply upward from both sides of the prison. Nearby the cold, shallow waters of the Lech rushed and gurgled over rocks and roots. From the generous double window of his cell Hitler enjoyed a charming view of lush gardens and the prisoners' recreation yard.

The prison at Landsberg was composed of two main sections. One was reserved for "normal" criminals; the other housed political prisoners like Hitler. Inside this second, so-called Festung section, Cell Number 7 was really two rooms: a living room and bedroom, furnished with a white iron bed, a nightstand, two chairs, a table, and a cupboard. Amid these surroundings, brightened with flowers, books, and well-wishers' gifts, Hitler received guests: friends, political cronies, businessmen, lawyers, journalists, publishers, and priests. When not watching inmate ball games from his windows or answering his mail, he went for walks in the gardens or held group discussions with his fellow Nazi inmates.

loyal Hess had escaped to Austria following the November putsch, only to return and surrender in order to be near his Führer. Now he dutifully took over the typing chores, and a familiar pattern began: Hitler sitting or pacing the cell floor voicing his thoughts and recollections, and Hess taking it all down.

As a politician, Hitler was more at home with oratory than with literature. "I know that men are won over less by the written than by the spoken word," he ventured in the preface, "that every great movement on this earth owes its growth to great orators and not to great writers. Nevertheless, for a doctrine to be disseminated [distributed] uniformly and coherently, its basic elements must be set down for all time."[41] With this principle in mind, Hitler proceeded to pour into his book, in a gushing torrent, all his political beliefs, his irrational prejudices and hatreds, and his twisted theory of Aryan superiority. *Mein Kampf* was to be the definitive statement of Hitler's weltanschauung—his view of life and the world. He did not intend to waste the opportunity.

Days at Landsberg followed typical routines. Promptly at 6:00 A.M. guards on the morning shift opened the cell doors. Breakfast was served at 7:00 in the inmates' "common room," usually coffee and porridge or bread. Between eight and ten o'clock prisoners were allowed to exercise in the courtyard or to stroll on the graveled walkways among the gardens. Afterward, mail was handed out and the inmates were allowed to pass the time as they wished until noon. At this time a modest dinner was served in the common room. Here Hitler's prominence among the convicts was clearly demonstrated. As John Toland tells it in *Adolf Hitler*: "The others waited behind their chairs until Hitler strode in, then someone called out, 'Attention!' He stood at the head of the table 'until every man in turn came forward with his table-greeting.' Politics was rarely discussed. Hitler usually chatted about theater, art or automobiles. After the meal they would smoke and gossip for quarter of an hour while the table was cleared, and then the Chief would retreat to his cell on the top floor to read, write in his diary or try to catch up on his correspondence."

Coffee or tea was served at 4:00 P.M., followed by more free time in the garden. The inmates took supper in their own cells at 6:00. After another period of exercise or meeting in the common room, lights were turned out at 10:00 P.M. Here in this not-so-Spartan atmosphere, Hitler wrote the first volume of *Mein Kampf*.

For three-and-a-half months, Hitler's labors continued. "All day long and late into the night," prison guard Franz Hemmrich reported, "one could hear the typewriter going in his room, and his voice dictating to Hess."[42] Work progressed steadily. "On Saturday evenings he usually read the finished passages to his fellow prisoners, who sat around him like disciples."[43] Finally, Hitler was ready to deliver the manuscript of Volume 1 to Max Amann. The Nazi publisher read it eagerly. What he had hoped for was a dramatic account of the inner workings of the party, complete with behind-the-scenes secrets and profiles of major party figures. What he got was a badly written and disjointed political and personal philosophy, lacking any real structure or style. It was not what Amann had expected—or wanted.

Nevertheless, he had promised to publish Hitler's book, and publish it he would. But first, at Amann's insistence, the author's long-winded title was reduced to its now familiar two-word length. To smooth out the cumbersome, rambling manuscript, a crew of Nazi figures took a hand in revising the text. They included Amann himself, Rudolf Hess, Ernst Hanfstängl, local music critic Josef Czerny, and Father Bernard Stempfle, an anti-Semitic priest. Together they corrected Hitler's grammar, reorganized his arrangement of topics, and toned down some of the more objectionable passages. Still it remained a verbose, heavily biased, and flawed book when it finally went to press.

A Deadly Vision Ignored

Despite all attempts to edit *Mein Kampf* into a readable form, the book suffers from a discouraging lack of order and organization. The text leaps almost carelessly from one topic to another in no particular sequence. Throughout its seven hundred pages, *Mein Kampf* mixes inflated autobiography with skewed history, ranting racism with jumbled political theory. Hitler's tone is by turns angry, philosophical, pompous, and resentful. The result is a meandering hodgepodge that is long-winded, clumsy, and often just plain dull.

Historians analyzing Hitler's strained and pretentious style of writing have characterized it as a cover-up for insecurity. It seems to indicate, writes Joachim C. Fest, "the anxiety of the half-educated author that his readers may question his intellectual competence. He tries to make his language imposing by stringing together long series of nouns . . . so that they sound empty and artificial."[44]

Nazi deputy Rudolf Hess was one of several men who revised and corrected the unwieldy Mein Kampf *manuscript.*

But for all its literary failings, *Mein Kampf* is significant in at least one respect. Among its rambling chapters Hitler lays bare his plans for the future with brazen honesty. The Nazi leader makes no secret of his raging hatred of Jews and Marxists, or his fervent belief that the German race was chosen by God to dominate all others. Nor does he shrink from brashly stating that a leader with a great vision is above the law, even when his will is carried out at the cost of innocent lives. Most remarkably, he states in plain words precisely *how* he intends to execute his ambitious schemes. Yet during the early years of the book's existence, few people paid attention to the ominous threat revealed in its text. In his introduction to one edition of *Mein Kampf*, Konrad Heiden explains:

> In its pages Hitler announced—long before he came to power—a program of blood and terror in a self-revelation of such overwhelming frankness that few among its readers had the courage to believe it. Once again it was demonstrated that there was no more effective method of concealment than the broadest publicity.[45]

The "self-revelations" that color the dark tapestry of *Mein Kampf* create the picture of a man obsessed with hate, bitter with jealousy, and striving to substitute cold ambition for the warmth of human relations. But even this portrait raises questions of its own. *Mein Kampf* does not fully explain what made Adolf Hitler the man he was. It says little regarding what forces and influences in his personal history combined to create his hatreds, his prejudices, his terrible drive to build by destroying. The answers to these questions must be found elsewhere. Fortunately, clues to the mystery can be found in the shadowy tangle of Hitler's early years.

Apprenticeship of an Anti-Semite

A host of voices from Hitler's past helped to shape the body of his beliefs. It seems clear that Hitler read little of the great European political and social thinkers, such as the French essayist Jean-Jacques Rousseau or the English philosopher John Locke. Nor did he ever study the original works of Germany's own Georg Hegel or Friedrich Nietzsche in any depth, if at all.

Instead, the young Hitler found an intellectual shortcut. Vienna in the early 1900s was a hotbed of individual political thought. Activists of all persuasions found they could reach the public with their ideas cheaply and effectively by publishing a pamphlet. Sold on city newsstands, these short booklets allowed authors to state their views with a maximum of rhetoric and, often, a minimum of reason. It was during this period that Hitler soaked up his erratic political "knowledge" from the pages of political pamphlets and local papers.

Many of these writings were unabashedly racist in content. One anti-Jewish pamphleteer who directly influenced Hitler's thinking was Guido von List. This anti-Semitic author was at his most prolific during the years Hitler lived in Vienna (1909–1913). List saw a dark threat looming on many fronts from "the hydra-headed international Jewish conspiracy."[46] How could Germany and Austria protect themselves

"Gradually I Began to Hate Them"

Anti-Semitism in Germany did not begin with Hitler; its roots in the fatherland stretched back for centuries. The young Austrian's personal descent into a lifelong loathing of the Jewish race was chronicled in some detail by Hitler himself in the pages of Mein Kampf. *He maintained his anti-Semitism developed after his 1909 arrival in Vienna. Here is Hitler's own version of his "transformation":*

"It is difficult, if not impossible, for me to say when the word 'Jew' first gave me ground for special thoughts. At home I do not remember having heard the word during my father's lifetime [Alois Hitler died in 1903]. . . . Not until my fourteenth or fifteenth year did I begin to come across the word 'Jew' with any frequency, partly in connection with political discussions . . . .

Then I came to Vienna . . . . In the first few weeks my eyes and my senses were not equal to the flood of [unfamiliar] values and ideas. Not until calm gradually returned and the agitated picture began to clear did I look around more carefully in my new world, and then among other things I encountered the Jewish question. . . .

For a few hellers I bought the first anti-Semitic pamphlets of my life . . . [now] Vienna appeared to me in a different light than before. Wherever I went, I began to see Jews, and the more I saw, the more sharply they became distinguished in my eyes from the rest of humanity."

from such a peril? First, List wrote, the nation must set up a racially pure state. Next, it must launch a global war to defeat these inferior yet threatening forces once and for all. At the same time a great leader would come forward to build a new Reich, free of racial impurities. The leader would be called "Arahari." The new Reich was to be divided into *Gaue,* or districts, each to be led by a *Gauleiter,* or leader. To keep the bloodlines pure, only Aryans would be permitted to be Reich citizens.

Where did the Aryan race derive its superior qualities? Here, List and others of his ilk called on a kind of scientific knowledge of race. Aryans, List declared, were possessed of a unique molecular structure of their blood. Moreover, the Aryans of old had handed down Aryan symbols that were as powerful as they were mysterious. These included the swastika and the double Sig runic letters "SS," which the

Hitler's distaste for Jewry grew deep and rabid. In his eyes the Jewish people became the source of all Germany's social and cultural ills, and leaders of the hated Social Democratic Party.

"I often grew sick to my stomach from the smell of these caftan-wearers . . . it became positively repulsive when, in addition to their physical uncleanliness, you discovered the moral stains on this 'chosen people' . . . .

Was there any form of filth or profligacy [reckless wastefulness], particularly in cultural life, without at least one Jew involved in it? If you cut even cautiously into such an abscess, you found, like a maggot in a rotting body, often bedazzled by the sudden light — a kike! What had to be reckoned heavily against the Jews in my eyes was when I became acquainted with their activity in the press, art, literature, and the theater. . . . This was pestilence [disease], spiritual pestilence, worse than the Black Death of olden times, and the people [were] being infected with it! . . .

I gradually became aware that the Social Democratic press was directed predominantly by Jews. . . . I took all the Social Democratic pamphlets I could lay hands on and sought the names of their authors: Jews. . . . Gradually I began to hate them. . . .

Hence today I believe I am acting in accordance with the will of the Almighty Creator: *by defending myself against the Jew, I am fighting for the work of the Lord.*"

Nazis would later adopt as insignia. Fortified with these qualities, Aryans were destined to seize control of the world.

"The Holy Grail of the German Blood"

Another pamphleteer, Jörg Lanz von Liebenfels, took the "reasoning" of List a step further. Writing in a publication called *Ostara*, Liebenfels called for a new order founded on racial purity. He espoused the theory that all men are divided into two groups, the "creative Aryans" and the "ape-men." In this new world, Aryans would be called upon to protect "the holy grail of the German blood."[47] Marriages between Aryans and the "inferior" races would be forbidden in order to guard against the "mongrelization"[48] of the Aryan race. The final step, according to Liebenfels, was the total elimination of Jews and other lesser races from the earth.

Whether Hitler actually read Liebenfel's work is unproven. Yet the fact that in *Mein Kampf* he used some of the same phrases Liebenfels used in his *Ostara* articles suggests that he might have. In his biography, *Adolf Hitler,* John Toland explores the possibility.

Ostara stirred in its readers the primal fear of the limitless power of the Jews—their control of money, their ascendancy

Depicting the "idealized" Aryan youth, a 1930s propaganda poster proclaims "The German Student" (upper left) and "Fight for the Führer and the People."

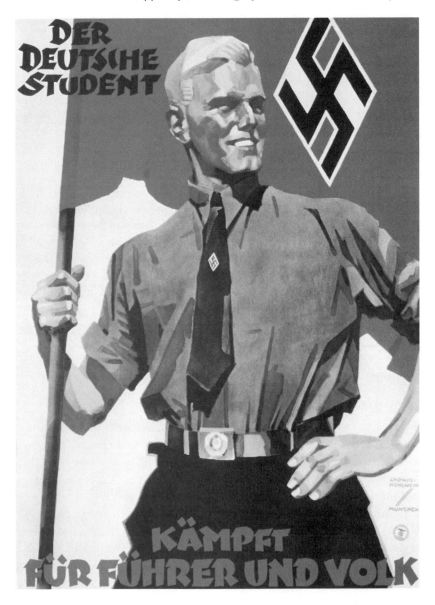

[rise] in the world of art and theater. How the erotic pictures in *Ostara* of blonde beauties embracing dark men must have inflamed Adolf! But as yet all these ideas were unrealized, unfocused.[49]

In time, and with the influence of like-minded men, Hitler's "ideas" would assume a darker, clearer form. What began as the idle questions of a dream-struck adolescent would harden into the rigid biases of a man who would later found a political movement based on hatred.

"One of the Best"

Following World War I, a number of zealous and often talented men crossed Hitler's path to influence and power. Two of the first were a Munich locksmith named Anton Drexler and Karl Harrer, a print journalist. Each had headed up his own political workers' party before merging in 1919 to become the German Workers' Party. Considered the actual founder of the National Socialist movement, it was Drexler who had pressed a pamphlet into Hitler's hands at the Austrian's first party meeting. Titled *My Political Awakening*, Drexler's pamphlet stirred sympathetic chords with the newcomer. Like Hitler, Drexler aimed to better the lives of the masses of working-class Germans, while scorning the values of the middle class.

Another addition to the growing list of Hitler's political mentors was Bavarian journalist and poet Dietrich Eckart. In contrast to Drexler, Eckart was credited with being the National Socialists' "spiritual" founder. He was well known on the Munich beer hall circuit for his articulate and fiery orations against the Jews and the Weimar Republic. In 1919 Eckart had expressed the need for a strong leader for the National Socialists, as related by William L. Shirer:

> We need a fellow at the head who can stand the sound of a machine gun. The rabble need to get fear into their pants. We can't use an officer, because the people don't respect them anymore. The best would be a worker who knows how to talk. . . . He doesn't need much brains.[50]

Twenty years his junior, Hitler was deeply impressed by Eckart's speeches and writings on Aryan superiority. For his part, Eckart saw in the fledgling politician the hope for a dynamic leader for the National Socialist movement. To groom Hitler for this role, Eckart coached him in his written and spoken German, toning down the Bavarian flavor of his speech. He also lent Hitler useful books and introduced him to his circle of friends. It was through Eckart that Hitler met Rudolf Hess, Alfred Rosenberg, and wealthy Germans eager to contribute to the party's coffers. Later, Hitler named Eckart editor of the *Völkischer Beobachter,* the Nazi newspaper. At the end of *Mein Kampf,* Hitler paid tribute to Eckart as "one of the best, who devoted his life to the awakening of his, our people, in his writings and his thoughts and finally in his deeds."[51]

Darwin and Others

The scope of Hitler's formal reading was somewhat limited. But the ideas of other writers and thinkers nonetheless infused his weltanschauung. The Austrian responded to the *words* of the composer Richard Wagner as much as his music. Beneath the surface of Wagner's operatic tributes to noble Teutonic heroes lurked an intense strain of anti-Semitism. "I hold the Jewish race to be the born enemy of pure humanity and everything noble in man,"[52] Wagner once wrote. Like Hitler, the composer of *Tristan und Isolde* and *Götterdämmerung* believed in a superior race (the Aryans) that subjugated and benefited from the labor of inferior races (particularly Jews and Slavs).

A famous friend of Wagner took this conviction a step further. Poet and philosopher Friedrich Nietzsche, one of the great German thinkers, was convinced that humanity was weak and adrift. Failed by religion, mired in conformity, the masses needed a special leader to lift them out of their aimless "slave morality." This savior could only be the *Übermensch*—the "overman," or superman. In a universe where God is dead, as Nietzsche claimed, the *Übermensch* would have the power to create new rules or values in *this* life, without concern for the next. There is little evidence that Adolf Hitler ever read *Beyond Good and Evil* or *The Will to Power* or any of Nietzsche's other books. And though he adamantly insisted on the supremacy of the state over the church, at no time did he reject outright the idea of God. Yet

Hitler corrupted the concept of the Übermensch introduced in the late 1800s by German philosopher Friedrich Nietzsche (pictured).

Lebensraum and
Freedom of Existence

"Only an adequately large space on this earth assures a nation of freedom of existence." In a single sentence from *Mein Kampf*, Hitler sums up the theory of lebensraum, or living space, as first formulated by fellow Nazi Alfred Rosenberg. Under this principle, a country was entitled to all the land it needed to ensure its greatness, no matter whose land it was. And which nations were entitled to this land? Again from *Mein Kampf*: "Nature as such has not reserved this soil for the future possession of any particular nation or race; on the contrary, this soil exists for the people which possesses the force to take it and the industry to cultivate it. Nature knows no political boundaries. First, she puts living creatures on this globe and watches the free play of forces. She then confers the master's right on her favorite child, the strongest in courage and industry."

Hitler's reference to Nature's "favorite child" was clear; he had only one country in mind as deserving the benefits of lebensraum: "We National Socialists must hold unflinchingly to our aim in foreign policy; namely, to secure for the German people the land and soil to which they are entitled on this earth."

Yet the boundaries of Germany were limited and confining. Where would this badly needed "land and soil" come from? To the west lay Germany's old neighbor and enemy, France. German National Socialists must stage "a final active reckoning with France" in which they would be "able to end the eternal and essentially so fruitless struggle between ourselves and France." And in the process, help themselves to all territory within the formerly French borders. Along with it could come the Sudetenland in Czechoslovakia, as well as Austria and western Poland. And what if room was needed to the east? The land there "could be obtained by and large only at the expense of Russia."

What would be the ultimate product of this policy? "No one can doubt that this world will some day be exposed to the severest struggles for the existence for mankind," he declares. "In the end, only the urge for self-preservation can conquer." In a strangely prophetic moment, Hitler seems to have predicted World War II itself.

Nietzsche's "superman" concept was easily distorted by the Nazis to support their idea of Aryan superiority. The philosopher's "will to power" theme—a way of gaining predominance over the weak and timid—became part of the Aryan identity.

Blended into this skewed mix of philosophies was a strained form of the theory of evolution. Proposed by Charles Darwin in his 1859 book *The Origin of Species,* the original theory sought to explain the rise of man from lower forms of life. A contemporary of both Wagner and Nietzsche, Darwin further stated that different species of animals remain in existence through a process called the "survival of the fittest." Those species that are strongest and adapt the most successfully are the species that survive. Like many of his fellows, Hitler believed deeply the notion that man and society undergo the same struggle. This twist on the evolutionary theory is called Social Darwinism. Hitler's brand of it placed German Aryans at the top of the evolutionary scale. The Nazis saw themselves as the "fittest" race on earth—which entitled them to dominate it.

Banking on Fear and Prejudice

Hitler liked to tout the National Socialist "philosophy" as one ordained by God. Yet history exposes Nazism as nothing more than a thinly veiled doctrine of arrogance, greed, and prejudice. Its policies were devised and executed solely to serve its preconceived hatreds and biases. Simply put, Hitler wanted to dominate the world; the "ideals" he followed were designed to help him do it. Hitler was obsessed by an irrational loathing of the Jews; distorting the philosophies of others gave him the excuse to persecute them.

Yet the Nazi Party was not alone in many of these beliefs. A significant number of German citizens agreed with much of what Hitler warned, threatened, or promised them. Hatred of the Jews, love of military might, and a longing for a return to glory were nothing new to them. "Nazism was not some terrible accident which fell out of a blue sky," wrote biographer Alan Bullock. "It was rooted in their history."[53] The wave of popular support that carried Hitler to power had its foundation in intellectual and cultural currents already well entrenched in German society.

Seeds of Evil

For all its author's guile and treachery, *Mein Kampf* was never deliberately vague. The book expressed Hitler's plans for a state-sponsored program of terrorism and mass murder with astonishing directness. Its anti-Semitic message was nothing new or obscure. *Mein Kampf* drew heavily upon philosophies both ancient and recent—and familiar to Old World thinking.

Distrust and hatred of Jews was nearly as old as Jewry itself. Many scholars believe this prejudice dates back at least as far as the crucifixion of Jesus Christ. In the view of the anti-Semites, Jesus—himself a Jew—was an innocent victim of the hatred of his own people. In his book *A History of the Holocaust*, Jewish historian Yehuda Bauer explains how this belief began.

> According to passages in the Gospels, [Jesus'] death at Roman hands was demanded by Judean [Jewish] supporters of the High Priest because he was seen as presenting himself as king of the Jews, or Messiah—a false Messiah, in Jewish eyes. This complicated story . . . was later interpreted by Christian anti-Semites as "proof" that "the Jews" had killed the Christ. This false myth of the Jews' supposed responsibility, one of the most destructive and murderous legends in human history, has whipped up passion and aggressions against a whole people and their civilization for many centuries.[54]

The Church and the Myth

The church fathers themselves were one reason for the persistence of this myth. In the centuries immediately following Jesus' death, church leaders routinely condemned the Jewish people. Some declared that Christianity had replaced Judaism in God's favor because the Jews had failed to accept Jesus as the Messiah. "Now the peoplehood of the Jews has been cancelled," wrote St. Cyprian in the third century A.D. "The Gentiles rather than the Jews will inherit the Kingdom."[55]

An even harsher view was held by St. John Chrysostom, a churchman of the Middle Ages. The Jews, he insisted, "had fallen into a condition lower than the vilest animals. Debauchery and drunkenness had brought them to the level of the lusty goat and the pig. They

Old World thinking held that Jesus (pictured at his crucifixion), was an innocent Jew hated by his own people, who betrayed him.

know only one thing: to satisfy their stomachs, get drunk and beat each other up. . . . It is the duty of all Christians to hate the Jews."[56]

Other European churchmen were more temperate. Church leaders such as St. Thomas Aquinas (1225–1274) and Protestant leader Martin Luther (1483–1546) may have favored persecuting and humiliating the followers of Judaism "because of their crime."[57] But they stopped short of advocating killing them. The Jews could still redeem themselves, these leaders said, but only if they gave up their birthright and converted to Christianity. Not surprisingly, few Jews were willing to do this.

The March of Anti-Semitism

One quality of Jews as a group that seemed threatening to others was their *differentness.* Author Samuel W. Mitcham Jr. describes the phenomenon in his book *Why Hitler?*

There is no doubt that Jews in the Middle Ages were distinct from other Europeans in terms of ancestry, religion, and culture; frequently they dressed differently as well. In an age that believed in magic and witchcraft, anyone who was different was suspect. The Jews were different: therefore, they were suspect.[58]

And they were suspected of much. Jews, it was alleged, stole blood from Christian babies and used it in demonic sacred rituals. It was

The Dark Side of a Monk from Wittenberg

"Know, Christian, that next to the devil thou hast no enemy more cruel, more venomous and violent than a true Jew."

These words—quoted by Lucy S. Dawidowicz in The War Against the Jews—*were penned by a most unlikely author. He was a descendant of peasants who became one of the most learned men of the sixteenth century. He was an Augustinian monk and teacher who—alone—dared challenge the might of the Church. He survived excommunication to write many learned works, including a German translation of the Bible. He was Martin Luther—best known for devising his Ninety-Five Theses in 1517 which paved the way for the rise of the Protestant Church. In 1542 he poured out his resentment and hatred of Jewry in a scathing pamphlet titled* Of the Jews and Their Lies *(as quoted in* A History of the Holocaust *by Yehuda Bauer):*

"First their synagogues or churches should be set on fire, and whatever does not burn up should be covered or spread over with dirt so that no one may ever be able to see a cinder or stone of it. . . . Secondly, their homes should likewise be broken down and destroyed. . . . Thirdly, they should be deprived of their prayerbooks and Talmuds. . . . Fourthly, their rabbis must be forbidden under threat of death to teach anymore. . . . If, however, we are afraid that they might harm us personally . . . then let us apply that same cleverness as the other nations, such as France, Spain, Bohemia, etc., and . . . drive them out of the country for all time."

In the 1920s and 1930s, Hitler and the Nazis would use Luther's anti-Semitism to validate their own. Not surprisingly, the works of Martin Luther enjoyed a resurgence of popularity during the Third Reich.

whispered that Jewish women sometimes gave birth to pigs instead of human babies. Far worse were the charges of tampering with the forces of nature. When the Black Death swept Europe in the late 1340s, superstitious citizens attributed the deadly plague to the work of Satan. Marked by their reputation as Christ-killers, the Jews were accused of being in league with the devil to cause the disaster. In retaliation, Europeans rose up and slaughtered hundreds of them.

The pressure placed on European Jews to convert to other faiths mounted steadily. When they refused, they were often answered with violent and sometimes deadly attacks called pogroms. As early as the seventh century, Muslim invaders tried to force Jews to convert to Islam. If they failed to comply, they were sometimes rounded up and massacred. Mass murders of Jews were more or less a regular occurrence in Spain of the Middle Ages. And Christian crusaders traveling to fight Muslims in the Holy Land (modern Israel) often stopped to murder "infidel" Jews along the way.

In this crude 1560 drawing, a Jew is depicted conjuring the devil from a pot of blood. Ignorant bigots of the time alleged that Jews stole the blood of Christian infants for such rituals.

When they were not slaughtered for their religion, hundreds of thousands of Jews were expelled from the nations in which they lived. One of the worst cases was the Spanish Expulsion of 1492. In this campaign, two hundred thousand Jews were made to leave the country. Additionally, Poland, France, Lithuania, and other countries forced Jews to flee to the Middle East, western Europe, British North America, and the islands of the Caribbean. Many never saw their native lands again.

Anti-Semitism in Modern Germany

Despite centuries of pogroms and expulsions, the Jewish population in Europe swelled to 1.25 million by 1755. By the mid–nineteenth century, Jews had become well assimilated in European society. A growing number held positions of prestige and learning as scientists, attorneys, doctors, and university professors. By the early 1930s, 26 percent of all lawyers in Germany were Jewish, as were 15 percent of all doctors. Longevity also worked to the advantage of the Jews. By the dawn of the twentieth century, Jewish people had lived in the region of Germany for more than sixteen hundred years.

Yet—or so many German Christians believed—it was a past without glory or historical tradition. With boundless pride, the Gentiles of Germany could point to their pre-Christian "golden age" of noble wars, valiant knights, and heroic legends. This romanticized heritage formed a major part of the nation's self-image. The Jews, they said, possessed no such heritage. "Unable to claim title to either Germanic or British pagan origins or the lores of the Christian knights," observed Yehuda Bauer, "the Jews were strangers who lived as second-class citizens in the countries of Europe."[59]

Then came World War I, the Great War of 1914–1918. The burden of shame and humiliation in the wake of Germany's defeat weighed heavily on her people. How, wondered the average German, could the armies of the kaiser have lost the war? Was theirs not a tradition of great and valiant warriors, destined to conquer and rule? Surely the conflict could not have been lost on the battlefield by the soldiers or generals. The blame, they were convinced, must lie elsewhere. It was only a matter of time before frustrated Germans searching for a scapegoat would target the Jews.

Their "reasoning" had a kind of misguided logic. The Jewish race, they believed, already had the blood of Jesus on its hands. That the Jews were allied with Satan and his demons was a widely accepted "fact." Never mind the fact that more than one hundred thousand Jews had fought for the fatherland in the war, or that ten thousand had died in the effort. What was more important was the "fact" that

Defeated German troops march home in 1918. Many of their countrymen bitterly resented Germany's loss and, looking for scapegoats, blamed the Jews.

the followers of Judaism had always been "outsiders," anxious to swindle German Gentiles and ravish their women. The Great War would have been their ideal opportunity to deal a deadly blow to Christian Germany.

A Wicked "Conspiracy"

It was not hard to imagine how the Jews would go about striking this blow. They would do it with the weapon they knew best, their enemies believed—money. After all, the German banking industry was surely "controlled" by Jews. And this was not merely a German operation, Hitler and others declared, but an international banking conspiracy. Jewish bankers in Germany and elsewhere made large loans of money to nations on *both* sides of the war; thus, *neither* side could become powerful enough to triumph. As the war progressed, lending institutions involved in this shameful "plot" began tightening Germany's credit so that its flow of money gradually dried up. Without adequate financing for the fatherland's war machine, Germany had little hope of winning the war. Even worse, anti-Semitic groups insisted, the Jews' shady lending practices helped to prolong the conflict merely to increase their profits.

Enemies of the Jews went ever further. To execute these dastardly schemes, the Jews of Germany and Europe might very well have recruited an ally. And who better than the standard-bearers of communism—that rising scourge born in Russia and now threaten-ing the very fabric of German life? Was it any coincidence that Karl Marx, Leon Trotsky, and other leaders of the hated Bolsheviks were Jews? The "evidence" seemed clear. "These facts, according to Hitler," wrote Samuel W. Mitcham Jr., "tied Judaism with commu-nism and proved that there was an international Jewish-Bolshevik

A Heroic Tradition in Myth and Music

Even at the time of Hitler's youth, the German empire had a centuries-old view of itself as a nation of fierce warriors and heroic traditions. This view did much to shape the national identity of the German people in the late nineteenth and early twentieth century. One artist who drew heavily on this theme was the prolific (if anti-Semitic) German composer Richard Wagner (1813–1883). In his book The Rise and Fall of the Third Reich, *journalist William L. Shirer de-scribes the influence of "this man of staggering genius."*

"Often a people's myths are the highest and truest expression of its spirit and culture, and nowhere is this more true than in Germany. . . . It was [Wagner's] towering operas, recalling so vividly the world of German antiquity with its heroic myths, its fighting pagan gods and heroes, its demons and dragons, its blood feuds and primitive tribal codes, its sense of destiny, of the splendor of love and life and the no-bility of death, which inspired the myths of modern Germany. . . .

It is the stupendous *Nibelungen Ring*, a series of four operas which is inspired by the great German epic myth, *Nibelunglied* . . . that gave Germany and especially the Third Reich so much of its primitive Ger-manic *mythos*. . . . Siegfried and Kriemhild, Brunhild and Hagen—these are the ancient heroes and heroines with whom so many mod-ern Germans liked to identify themselves. With them, and with the world of the barbaric pagan Nibelungs—an irrational, heroic, mystic world, beset by treachery, overwhelmed by violence, drowned in blood . . . which has always fascinated the German mind and answered some terrible longing in the German soul. . . . In that German soul could be felt the struggle between civilization and the spirit of the Ni-belungs, and in the time with which this history is concerned the lat-ter seemed to gain the upper hand. . . .

From his earliest days Hitler worshiped Wagner, and even as his life neared a close . . . he loved to reminisce about all the times he had heard the great Wagnerian works, of what they meant to him."

conspiracy, whose aim was to dominate and enslave Germany and, indeed, the entire world."[60]

In more ordinary times, these wild accusations might have had little effect on the German populace. But the times were far from ordinary. Germany in the 1920s and 1930s was a proud, nationalistic society that had been reduced by the Great War to licking its wounds and searching for excuses. The clumsy but well-intentioned efforts of the Weimar Republic to deal with hard times and bring order to Germany were failing. Because of their differentness, financial prosperity, and professional success, the Jews were an easy target for suspicion, jealousy, and blame. Adolf Hitler mirrored the extreme view of many Germans when he wrote in *Mein Kampf*:

> If at the beginning of the war, and during the war, twelve or fifteen thousand of these Hebrew corrupters of the people had been held under poison gas, as happened to hundreds of thousands of our very best German workers in the field, the sacrifice of millions at the front would not have been in vain. On the contrary: twelve thousand scoundrels eliminated in time might have saved the lives of a million real Germans, valuable for the future.[61]

The Jew had become the inevitable *Sündenbock,* or scapegoat, for the Great War and everything else that was wrong with Germany. And the German people were only too willing to believe it.

The *Völkisch* Idea

The thread of racism ran freely through all of Hitler's philosophy. It formed the basis for the *völkisch* idea, a mythology that drew together the themes of racial purity, Aryan superiority, and lebensraum. The *Volk* were not simply one nationality or population. They were a special tribal people with close ties to the soil, selected by natural forces for a noble fate. "Nature," Hitler explained in *Mein Kampf,* "confers the master's right on her favorite child, the strongest in courage and industry."[62] Nature's "favorite child," of course, was the Aryan race. And their special destiny was nothing short of world domination.

In the *völkisch* view, all men were *not* created equal. Its philosophy "by no means believes in an equality of the races," Hitler wrote. Instead, "it recognizes their higher or lesser value and feels itself obligated . . . to promote the victory of the better and stronger, and demand the subordination of the inferior and weaker."[63] By virtue of its "pure" blood and warrior heritage, the Aryan race was fated to be the better and stronger. Actually, the "Aryans" were not a true race in the

Hitler's vicious racism colored all of German society. Here, a placard affixed to a Jewish store proclaims: "Germans, defend yourselves! Do not buy from Jews!"

scientific sense. The term referred to an idealized physical image—tall, fair-skinned, and superior by birth—that provided the model for the Nazi "master race."

The special destiny of this exalted people faced only one danger: the Jews. To Hitler, the religious practices of the Jewish people were never any threat to the Nazis' plans. The real threat, he believed, came from his view of the Jews as a race—an inferior, subhuman species capable of fouling the purity of Aryan blood. To prevent this racial "pollution," the *völkisch* philosophy forbade the marriage of German Gentiles and Jews. In time, this strategy would progress first to the removal, and later the total elimination, of the Jew.

Once he came to power, Hitler would religiously follow the road mapped out for him by his *völkisch* ideology. In the words of William L. Shirer, "he would unify a chosen people who had never before been politically one. He would purify their race. He would make them strong. He would make them lords of the earth."[64]

Missed Opportunities

If the ideas in *Mein Kampf* struck familiar chords with the German populace, the same cannot be said of government leaders throughout the world. In fact, statesmen of many nations found it difficult to take Adolf Hitler seriously at all—at first. To politicians and citizens alike, the future German chancellor even seemed something of a joke, with his quaint mustache, smallish stature and the wild theatrics of his speechmaking. Yet the dark messages of *Mein Kampf* are plainly stated in its pages, however disorganized or badly phrased they may be. In his biography *The Life and Death of Adolf Hitler,* Robert Payne takes up this point.

> The Germans who did not trouble to read the book and the politicians outside Germany who dismissed it as a turgid [grandiose] and repetitious political tract made a great mistake. Few people read it attentively, and there is no evidence that [Stanley] Baldwin, [Neville] Chamberlain, [Winston] Churchill, [Franklin D.] Roosevelt, [Joseph] Stalin, or any of the political leaders most directly affected did anything more than glance at it. If they had read it with the attention it deserves, they would have seen what was a blueprint for the total destruction of bourgeois [upper middle class] society and the conquest of the world.[65]

Prejudice in Their Own Backyards

It was easy for the world's leaders of the 1920s and early 1930s to turn a blind eye to the rising Nazi threat. After all, the "Jewish question" seemed to cause little trouble outside of Germany. Besides, with the global crisis brought on by the Great Depression of the 1930s, most governments had their hands full just coping with financial problems in their own backyards.

Indeed, at first glance, conditions for the followers of Judaism might not have seemed all that grim. In many European nations, Jews made up less than 2 percent of the population and experienced some degree of acceptance into society and the workplace. The Jews

Who Read *Mein Kampf?*

When it was first published in 1925, Mein Kampf was not a run-away bestseller. No crowds stampeded the bookstalls and newsstands; no fans clamored for the author's autograph. The reason: Despite his brief national notoriety during his 1924 trial for treason, Hitler was still an obscure political figure. Konrad Heiden explains it this way in his introduction to one edition of the "Nazi bible."

"Adolf Hitler, the author of *Mein Kampf*, was not yet Adolf Hitler, the Führer of Germany; he lacked the experience, the responsibilities, the knowledge. In fact, he was nothing more than an organizer of street fights, an impresario [director] of mass meetings, the leader of a virtually non-existent party."

American correspondent William L. Shirer arrived in Germany during the late 1920s. He observes in The Rise and Fall of the Third Reich *that even then the future führer was not taken too seriously. "One scarcely heard of Hitler or the Nazis except as butts of jokes, usually in connection with the Beer Hall Putsch, as it came to be known." Yet in* Mein Kampf *'s first year of publication it sold just under ninety-five hundred copies. Someone was buying it—but who was reading it?*

Hardly anyone, according to William L. Shirer: "Not every German who bought a copy of Mein Kampf *necessarily read it. I have heard many a Nazi stalwart complain that it was hard going, and not a few admit—in private—that they were never able to get through to the end of its 783 turgid [overwritten] pages." Although sales of* Mein Kampf *rose proportionately with Hitler's rise to power, there is little evidence that it was widely read even then. In fact, the Führer was never to win much respect as a writer even from his supporters. "The average party member did not read the book," writes Konrad Heiden. "And among the leaders it was a common saying that Hitler was an extraordinary speaker, a great leader, a political genius, but 'it's too bad he had to write that silly book.'"*

In later years the author himself weighed in on his literary creation. Biographer John Toland relates in his book Adolf Hitler *that Hitler "admitted to [Nazi attorney Hans] Frank that he was no author. 'Thoughts run away from me when I write.'* Mein Kampf, *he admitted, was merely a collection of lead articles for the* Völkischer Beobachter. *'Of one thing I am sure; if I had known in 1924 that I would become Chancellor, I would not have written the book.'"*

of the Netherlands, France, and Luxembourg, for example, enjoyed full civic equality. The intermarriage of Christian and Jewish Italians actually rose during the 1930s. And the Belgian government went so far as to grant funds for the relief of Jewish refugees from Germany. But beneath this deceptively integrated surface, worldwide racism and anti-Semitism seethed. French Jews were harassed by right-wing extremist groups such as the Action Française, which was convinced Jews were behind a national conspiracy. Despite Britain's general acceptance of Jews, many middle- and upper-class Britons suspected that international Jewry was tied to bolshevism. In strife-torn Poland, home to a Jewish population of nearly 3 million, Jew-haters mounted a regular succession of deadly pogroms throughout the 1930s. The misery and squalor in which Polish Jews lived prompted one Jewish American writer to describe them as "buried alive."[66]

The United States was hardly free of anti-Semitism, either. A series of polls conducted in 1940—before America's entry into World War II—showed that nearly 20 percent of Americans viewed Jews as a national menace. Anti-Jewish organizations had been a fixture on the American landscape for decades. One was the Silver Shirts, an anti-Semitic group active during the 1930s, which warned that the United States had been infiltrated by 7 million Jewish Communists. Prominent individuals added their voices to the racist din, as well.

In the 1940s, many Americans were anti-Semitic, including "radio priest" Father Charles E. Coughlin.

Perhaps the best known was "radio priest" Father Charles E. Coughlin, who maintained that Jewish Communists controlled the American financial system and short-changed U.S. workers.

A greater blemish on the nation's race relations lay in its often violent conflict between black and white Americans. In 1932 alone, angry whites seized and lynched twenty-eight African Americans across the Deep South. The racist organization Ku Klux Klan enjoyed higher popularity during this era than at any time since Reconstruction (1865–1877). Neither the United States nor Europe could claim spotless records on matters of ethnicity and race. Perhaps this was one reason they found it easy to delay condemning Nazi Germany for its treatment of the Jews.

Mussolini and Italian Fascism

Not all of Adolf Hitler's political influences dated back centuries or even decades. One had come into national power in Italy only a year before Hitler's ill-fated 1923 putsch.

An Italian schoolteacher and journalist by trade, Benito Mussolini was a Socialist by philosophy. But during World War I he turned away from socialism and was expelled from his party. Quickly rebounding, he and like-minded colleagues formed the Fasci di Combattimento in March 1919. The new party took its name from the emblem of ancient Roman authority, the fasces—a bundle of sticks tied to an ax. In 1922 the Fascist Party seized power in Rome and Mussolini declared himself Il Duce, the leader.

Italian fascism had much in common with Hitler's Nazi philosophy. Like Germany's National Socialists, the Fascists in Italy believed in a totalitarian, single-party government under an absolute dictator. Both parties exalted military power and feared the spread of communism. Like Hitler, Mussolini was a dynamic orator and demagogue who did not shrink from eliminating political rivals. But while the Führer appealed most to German workers and the lower class, Il Duce openly curried favor with the Italian upper classes, big business, and the army. There was another way in which the two leaders differed. "Unlike Hitler . . . [Mussolini] did not pretend that the Italians were a master race," writes Mark Arnold-Forster in *The World at War.* "His philosophy did not tell him that he was destined to dominate Europe or anywhere else in particular. In foreign affairs Mussolini's chief motive was greed."[67]

Still, Hitler had been sufficiently impressed by Mussolini's 1922 march on Rome to mention him in *Mein Kampf:*

> In this period . . . I conceived the profoundest admiration for the great man south of the Alps, who, full of ardent love for his people, made no pacts with the enemies of Italy, but strove for their annihilation by all ways and means. What will rank Mussolini among the great men of this earth is his determination not to share Italy with the Marxists [Communists], but to destroy internationalism and save the fatherland from it.[68]

Despite the rise of fascist movements in Spain, Japan, France, and other countries during the 1920s and 1930s, it was Italian fascism that Hitler embraced. In Mussolini, he thought he could see a strong and effective future ally.

Hitler admired Italy's Fascist dictator Benito Mussolini (right). Both men possessed charismatic traits; both were brutal dictators.

Hitler's Influences Versus Hitler's Beliefs

For the most part, the factors and philosophies that shaped Hitler's thinking were neither groundbreaking nor revolutionary. He was deeply influenced by the frustrations, fears, and prejudices that marked centuries-old European attitudes. He was, to a large extent, a product of his place and times. Where Hitler differed from his fellow Germans and Austrians seems to be in the way his mind filtered the ideas he acquired. He appeared to absorb only those attitudes which were negative and destructive. Any positive or productive ideas which he processed were apparently ignored or discarded.

Mein Kampf was the ultimate expression—if a crude one—of Hitler's "education." But perhaps it was not surprising that world leaders in the mid-1920s took small notice of the book. A windy, pretentious tome, authored by the jailed leader of a banned political party, was unlikely to draw the attention of those in high places. It was a fatal oversight. In the next two decades, Hitler was to show them exactly what they missed.

Implementing a National Policy of Hatred

Many resolutions made in prison fade into dim memory once the prisoner again tastes freedom. But never for a moment did Adolf Hitler lose sight of the beliefs and ambitions he voiced in *Mein Kampf*. From that point on he labored to implement the prejudice and hatreds that motivated him so fiercely: rampant anti-Semitism, an obsession for living space for his Nazi regime, and an insatiable thirst for power. If at times he found it necessary to deviate from his path, the detours were only temporary. He inevitably returned to the precepts expressed in the book he had begun behind the ancient walls of Landsberg Prison.

The Publication of *Mein Kampf*

Five days before Christmas 1924, Hitler received an early holiday gift. Thanks to the intervention of three sympathetic judges from his trial, he was abruptly paroled. On the same day, Hitler left the facility, where he had spent thirteen months, a free man. Seven months later, as he labored on his second volume, the first portion of *Mein Kampf* was published.

Volume 1—all four hundred pages—appeared in the summer of 1925. The book sold for the sum of twelve marks, the equivalent of about three dollars, a copy. Public reaction was disappointing. Despite Max Amann's boast of initial sales of twenty-three thousand copies, *Mein Kampf* sold fewer than ninety-five hundred copies in its first year. The publication of the three-hundred-page Volume 2 in December 1926 did little to boost its dwindling sales over the next two years.

Yet as Hitler's political star began rising once again, so did the success of his book. By the time he became chancellor of Germany in 1933, *Mein Kampf* was racking up sales of 1 million copies per year. By 1940, 6 million copies had been sold. The royalties it earned made Hitler wealthy.

Rebuilding the Nazi Party

For the newly released Nazi leader, however, there was much to do. Now living in Munich, according to William L. Shirer, Hitler found

Hitler's Book

The fortunes of Mein Kampf *rose and fell with the fortunes of its author and his Nazi Party. Shortly after its initial publication in 1925—the first full year after Hitler's release from prison—the first volume sold a modest 9,473 copies. In December of the following year, Volume 2 of* Mein Kampf *was published. But few people outside the Nazi Party took notice. For the next three years sales dropped steadily. The book—and its ex-convict author—seemed to hold little attraction for the majority of Germans.*

In 1929, as the presence of the Nazi Party grew stronger, Mein Kampf's *sales began to take off, reaching a respectable 7,664 copies. The turning point came in 1930. The Great Depression was well underway, and the German people struggled to cope with falling employment, rising hunger, and greater fears for the future. Their faith in the power of the Weimar Republic to deliver them from this crisis fell lower with each passing month. As they groped in the economic darkness for relief from their suffering, many Germans grasped at the first political figure who offered them hope. That figure was Adolf Hitler; his party was the Nazi Party; his book was* Mein Kampf. *That year, a less costly, single-volume edition was released, and sales soared to 54,000 copies.*

As Hitler's visibility and popularity swelled, so did purchases of his book. When Hitler became chancellor in 1933, resulting sales of one million copies propelled Mein Kampf *into the ranks of all-time best-sellers. And, as William L. Shirer reports in* The Rise and Fall of the Third Reich, *it would remain one.*

"Except for the Bible, no other book sold as well during the Nazi regime, when few families felt secure without a copy on the table. It was almost obligatory—and certainly politic—to present a copy to a bride and groom at their wedding, and nearly every school child received one on graduation from whatever school. By 1940, the year after World War II broke out [in Europe], six million copies of the Nazi bible had been sold in Germany."

a situation which would have led almost any other man to retire from public life. The Nazi Party and its press were banned, the former leaders were feuding and falling away. Hitler himself was forbidden to speak in public. What was worse, he faced deportation to his native Austria. . . . Even many of his old comrades agreed with the general opinion that Hitler was finished, that now he would fade away into oblivion.[69]

But Hitler's term in prison had only strengthened his resolve. His first great challenge was to restore his party to the national political scene. First, he persuaded the prime minister of Bavaria to lift the ban on the Nazi Party. But on the next step, he stumbled. In a speech to four thousand Nazi regulars in Munich, he denounced the use of violence to achieve the party's ends. The speaker's platform and the ballot box, he urged, should be the Nazi path to prominence. Apparently forgetting his promise of nonviolence, he added, "To this struggle of ours there are only two possible issues: either the enemy passes over our bodies or we pass over theirs!"[70]

Noting the threat spelled out in the Austrian's statements, Bavarian authorities promptly banned him from further public speaking. Despite this setback, Hitler was far from idle. He busied himself renewing contacts with Nazi leaders, raising funds, and contributing articles for the *Völkischer Beobachter,* the Nazi newspaper. Hitler believed his day would come. For the present, he was content to work behind the scenes and wait for the right moment.

Making the Most of Crisis

The mid-1920s were not favorable to the Nazi cause. The bleak years following World War I had provided fertile soil for the seeds of the National Socialist Party. "It had mushroomed on the country's misfortunes," William L. Shirer observed. "Now that the nation's outlook was suddenly bright it was rapidly withering away."[71] By the 1928 elections, the quality of life was improving steadily; inflation had eased and more people were working. The average German saw little need for a party that promised radical change.

October 1929 brought the crisis Hitler had been waiting for. In the United States, the New York stock market collapsed, marking the start of the Great Depression. This worldwide phenomenon of economic failure, soaring unemployment, hunger, and loss soon rippled into Germany. The country's rising prosperity crumbled.

The nation's renewed economic problems revived the popularity of radical political factions. Chief among these was the Communist Party. Military leaders looked anxiously to the Weimar government for help in controlling the Communist elements. The republic's president was now the aging hero of World War I, Field Marshall Paul von Hindenburg. A distinctive figure in his gray crewcut and handlebar mustache, Hindenburg shared power with his chancellor, Hermann Müller. The greatest challenge facing the popular president was to keep both the Communists and the Nazis out of power.

By 1930, however, the Nazis had won enough seats to become the second largest party in the Reichstag. In October 1931 Hitler attempted to woo Hindenburg himself. But the German president was not impressed by the Nazi leader or his ambitions. "This Bohemian corporal wants to become Reich chancellor?" Hindenburg snorted to his lieutenants after the interview. "Never!"[72]

Yet the following year Hindenburg found himself running against the same "Bohemian corporal" in his bid for reelection. The president only narrowly defeated Hitler in the voting. If nothing else, the campaign had given Hitler the opportunity to heighten his credibility as a "serious" politician. In the next election, the Nazi Party rode its wave of rising popularity to become Germany's largest political party.

German president Paul von Hindenburg struggled to keep both the Nazis and the Communists out of power.

All the while, Hindenburg faced mounting pressure to name Hitler chancellor of Germany. Fearful of the ruthlessness of Nazi methods, the president resisted. But Hitler's public popularity was undeniable. Eighty-five years old, ailing, and weary of politics, President von Hindenburg finally gave in. Around noon on January 30, 1933, Hitler was sworn in as Reichschancellor of Germany.

Consolidating Power

"There must be no majority decisions," Hitler had declared in *Mein Kampf*, "but only responsible persons. . . . Surely every man will have advisers by his side, but *the decisions will be made by one man*"[73] The new chancellor lost no time in acting in line with this so-called Führer Principle of despotic rule. In a crucial first step, he used a loophole article in the Weimer

The ailing Hindenburg (left) rides in an open car with the new chancellor of Germany. The German president reluctantly appointed Hitler to the post in January 1933 as coalition after coalition failed to stabilize the government.

Constitution, allowing the president extraordinary powers during times of national crisis, to force through parliament two crucial pieces of legislation designed to wrest authority from the German people and place it in his own hands.

On February 27 the Reichstag building mysteriously caught fire and was destroyed. A Dutch Communist was arrested for starting the blaze. Hitler seized upon the episode to convince Hindenburg to approve a "defensive measure against Communist acts of violence endangering the state."[74] In reality, the new decree repealed seven sections of the German constitution that guaranteed personal and civil liberties—for *all* Germans. No longer did citizens enjoy the rights of freedom of speech, of assembly, or a free press. At any time they could be searched, or their telephone or mail communications could be monitored.

The second law—the Law for the Removal of the Distress of People and State—stripped the Reichstag of its authority to create laws, approve treaties, and control the budget. This so-called Enabling Act handed over all these powers to the Reich cabinet and chancellor. Hitler took no chances with the final vote. He ordered his agents to intimidate and even arrest any politician who opposed the bill. To further cement his authority, Hitler next abolished all other political parties. For the next twelve years, the Nazis would be the sole governing force in Germany.

In 1934 Hitler cleaned his own house in the infamous "Blood Purge." In one weekend of incredible ruthlessness he had an estimated eighty-five people—most of them Nazis—murdered for opposing his policies. Now only one obstacle stood between Hitler and unfettered power. On August 2, 1934, Hindenburg died at the age of eighty-six. Hitler immediately combined the two offices of president and chancellor under the title of Führer. At the same time, he forced military leaders to swear personal allegiance directly to him instead of the state. "From the smallest community cell to the highest leadership of the entire Reich," Hitler had written in *Mein Kampf*, "the state must have the personality [Führer] principle anchored in its organization."[75] Under its weight the crumbling and discredited Weimar Republic at last gave way to the Third Reich. And Adolf Hitler was its undisputed master, finally powerful enough to implement the ideas he had expressed in *Mein Kampf* a decade earlier.

Hitler Rearms Germany

One of his greatest goals grew out of his bitterness over the terms of the Treaty of Versailles. The new Führer was not content for the Third Reich to merely exist. As part of Hitler's "New Order" the Reich had to grow, to expand, to dominate. To accomplish this, he had stated in *Mein Kampf*, Nazi Germany must be free of the "boundless repression" of the Treaty of Versailles. Then he had added a solemn warning: *"Peace treaties whose demands are a scourge to nations [often] strike the first roll of drums for the uprising to come."*[76] In direct defiance of the treaty Hitler quietly began his campaign to rearm the fatherland.

War had brought about the despised treaty that so oppressed the German people. War, Hitler believed, was the only method by which he could return Germany to its full glory. But, surrounded by hostile nations, he would have to move carefully. Once again, Hitler relied on deceit to disguise his real intentions to the world. To both the French and British press he spoke eloquently of the need for peace. Meanwhile, plans to secretly rearm Germany were already in motion.

Under strictest secrecy, Hitler ordered the German army to triple its manpower from one hundred thousand to three hundred thousand men by October 1, 1934. To his second in command, Hermann Göring, Hitler awarded the task of rebuilding the Luftwaffe, or German air force. At the same time, the navy began construction of two battle cruisers of twenty-six thousand tons, more than twice the limit allowed by the Versailles treaty. Submarines, strictly forbidden by the treaty, were already being assembled in Finland, Holland, and Spain.

By the end of 1934 word of Hitler's treaty violations had spread across Europe. Neighboring countries issued half-hearted diplomatic protests, but took no punitive action. Emboldened, Hitler reestablished the German military draft in March 1935. His goal: an army of thirty-six divisions for a total of a half-million men. "That was the end of the military restrictions of Versailles," observed William L. Shirer, "unless France and Britain took action. As Hitler expected, they protested but they did not act."[77]

The Jewish Question

In these lines from *Mein Kampf,* Hitler clearly defined the relationship between the Jew and the Aryan: evil versus good; the *Untermensch,* or subhuman, versus the *Übermensch,* or superman:

Hitler charged Hermann Göring with secretly rebuilding the German air force, which was officially banned by the Treaty of Versailles. Here, Luftwaffe bombers fly over a Nuremberg rally in a display of military might.

The mightiest counterpart to the Aryan is represented by the Jew. . . . In his vileness he becomes so gigantic that no one need be surprised if among our people the personification of the devil as the symbol of all evil assumes the living shape of the Jew. [78]

Ridding Germany of Jews was not merely a part of Hitler's New Order; it was the cornerstone. He was convinced that the Jews, like the Nazis, also had a grand scheme to dominate the world. The chief difference was that the Jews would dominate Europe under the Communist banner, the Germans under the swastika. The outcome of this struggle was critical. "If, with the help of his Marxist [Communist] creed," Hitler had warned in *Mein Kampf*, "the Jew is victorious over the other peoples of the world, his crown will be the funeral wreath of humanity."[79]

Now that he was führer, Hitler was free to unleash his unholy war against European Jewry. An all-out frontal assault, he knew, would bring down a storm of international criticism. Making the Third Reich *Judenfrei* (free of Jews) would have to be a gradual process. On April 1, 1933, the Nazis enacted a one-day nationwide boycott of all Jewish businesses and professions. Brown-shirted SA squads swarmed into the streets of cities throughout Germany. They painted yellow Stars of David on the doors and windows of Jewish establishments, adding slogans such as "Jew, Die!" Troopers posted at doorways bore signs warning Germans not to patronize Jewish shops. Hitler's next blow was aimed not at their pocketbooks, but at their intellects. On May 10, Propaganda Minister Joseph Goebbels staged book burnings in locations all across Germany. Thousands of books written by Jewish, Communist, and other "undesirable" authors went up in flames.

Within days of the boycott, the Reich ordered the forced "retirement" of all non-Aryan government workers and forbade German Jews to serve as lawyers, judges, physicians, or dentists. Additional laws barred Jews from teaching in universities or working in films, live theater, or radio. The Nuremberg Laws of 1935 mounted a still greater assault on their personal liberties. The first of these decrees, the Reich Citizenship Law, robbed the Jews of their status as German citizens. From now on, Jewish people would be officially recognized as nothing more than "subjects."

The second decree, the Law for the Protection of German Blood and German Honor, echoed in its opening words Hitler's belief that "the purity of German blood is a prerequisite for the continued existence of the German people."[80] Its provisions barred Jews from marrying or having sexual relations with non-Jews. Employing Gentile women of childbearing age in Jewish households was also forbidden.

Instigated by Propaganda Minister Joseph Goebbels, Nazi book burnings such as this destroyed thousands of books by Jews, Communists, and other targeted authors.

In 1936 the Reich took yet another step by initiating the Four-Year Plan. Under this scheme, Jewish business owners who could no longer operate under the Reich's racial laws were offered an alternative. To escape their financial dilemma, they could sell their businesses to the Nazis for a cut-rate price. This scheme was designed to impoverish Jews while it lined the pockets of high-ranking Nazi officials.

Then the proceedings took a sudden and violent turn. The murder of a German diplomat in Paris by a young Polish Jew gave the Reich the excuse for an unprecedented act of violence. The night of November 9, 1938, was selected as the date; the homes, businesses, and synagogues of Jews were the targets. At the appointed time, waves of SS men and Gestapo agents in civilian clothes swarmed into the streets of cities all across Germany. They smashed windows, looted shops and homes, and publicly beat and even murdered their Jewish owners. At least two hundred synagogues were broken into, ransacked, and set ablaze. The terror of this *Kristallnacht*—"Night of Broken Glass"—sparked the outrage of many German citizens. For the Nazis, it marked the beginning of a more systematic and brutal program for dealing with the Jews.

Lebensraum in Action

If Hitler was obsessed with eradicating the Jews, he was equally as driven to ensure lebensraum—living space—for the Aryan race. In his mind the two obsessions had become closely linked. John Toland explains the Führer's twisted reasoning this way: "If the Reich failed to acquire essential living space it would perish. If the Jewish menace were not stemmed there could be no struggle for *Lebensraum*, no culture, and the nation would decay."[81]

Hitler had clearly stated his beliefs regarding lebensraum in *Mein Kampf*. "For Germany, consequently, the only possibility for carrying out a healthy territorial policy [lies] in the acquisition of new land in Europe itself."[82] In early 1936 Hitler jealously eyed the Rhineland. This stretch of German territory bordering France, Belgium, and the

Everyday Life in the "New Order"

By the mid-1930s, the worst days of the Great Depression were behind the people of Germany. The Nazi Party seemed to be delivering the sorely needed relief it promised from the chaos spawned by hard times and the failures of the Weimar Republic. Citizens began enjoying a nearly forgotten sense of security. So engrossed were Christian Germans in their own improving fortunes that they scarcely noticed the dismantling of the civil rights of Jews. Nor did they seem to mind the gradual erosion of their own freedoms. The streets were quiet, people were working, and poverty was disappearing. If living in a police state was the price Germans paid for this "New Order," most were willing to pay it—at first.

Organization was the key. It was mandated by the Führer and enforced by his special security forces: the Schutzstaffel, or SS, and its secret political arm, the Geheime Staatspolizei, or Gestapo. Under Nazi rule, every phase of life was strictly regimented. Each citizen— of every age and walk of life—fitted (or was made to fit) into a particular slot in a network of party organizations designed to serve the state. As early as age four, German children were taught the National Socialist way of thinking in grade school. For most, the next step was entry into some branch of the Hitlerjugend, the Hitler Youth. In groups like the Jungvolk and Jungmädel, boys and girls were drilled in physical fitness, "racial science," and, above all, unquestioning loyalty to their Führer.

Hitler's New Order kept its citizens on a short leash. Devotion to the Nazi philosophy was demanded; willingness to report and betray anyone who disagreed was encouraged. Those who dared to challenge

Netherlands had been clear of German military forces since the Versailles treaty of 1919. Hitler wanted it back and he wanted it armed. On March 7 he ordered troops to march into the Rhineland and occupy it. Surprisingly, French military forces did not retaliate. Hitler had taken possession of the region without firing a shot.

In the same bloodless fashion, Hitler accomplished his *Anschluss*—the reunification of Germany and his homeland of Austria—in March 1938. In October the Führer sent troops into the heavily German Sudetenland section of Czechoslovakia. Five months later, the Nazis annexed the rest of Czechoslovakia—again, without the use of violence.

"The right to possess soil can become a duty if without extension of its soil a great nation seems doomed to destruction," Hitler had

Reich policy often were arrested by the secret police, taken away, and never seen again. Their disappearance was justified by official orders that decreed the fate of persons who "endangered German security" was to vanish without a trace into the "night and fog." The fear created by the SS and Gestapo changed the way Germans—especially Jews—thought, felt, and lived their everyday lives. In his book SS and Gestapo: Rule by Terror, *Roger Manvell describes the effects of this climate of fear:*

"The ordinary citizen . . . soon learns to pay lip-service to the regime, and keep his nose clean. He does his daily job, performs his military service, wears the prescribed badges, pays the right dues, gives the right salutes, and keeps quiet about anything dubious he may know or suspect is going on. . . . He has learned always to be wary of strangers, wary of his friends, wary even of the members of his family, more especially the younger generation who have been warned to watch their parents. Above all, he is careful to let slip nothing which might be held politically suspect . . . and he shies away from acquiring any knowledge which could conceivably be judged as dangerous."

This day-in and day-out routine of suspicion and fear took a terrible toll on many Germans. They became passive, distrustful, and too frightened to join together to resist the Nazi regime—ironically, the opposite of the proud and strong "Aryan" ideal that Hitler envisioned his Greater German Reich would produce.

Passersby view the devastation wrought by SS agents and other Nazi supporters in a violent spasm of anti-Semitism on Kristallnacht.

written in Volume 2 of *Mein Kampf.* "Germany will either be a world power or there will be no Germany."[83] The Führer seemed well on his way to ensuring the first possibility and preventing the second.

The Reich at War

Now Hitler set his sights on Poland. To bolster its own military strength, Germany signed alliances with both Italy's Fascist dictator Benito Mussolini and Soviet dictator Joseph Stalin. Then on September 1, 1939, Nazi forces charged into Poland, their tanks and warplanes pounding her farms, villages, and cities. Two days later, France and Britain declared war on Germany and World War II began.

In the spring and summer of 1940, the Nazi blitzkrieg easily overran Belgium and the Netherlands. France was the next to fall, surrendering after only five weeks of fighting. England fared somewhat better. Despite a deadly series of air strikes by Göring's Luftwaffe, designed as a preliminary to the German invasion of Great Britain, the British managed to fend off the Nazis. While the rest of the world watched Hitler's aggression with growing concern, few outsiders had any inkling of the "secret war" boiling beneath the surface.

The Secret War: Expulsion and Enclosure

The fall of Poland served two immediate purposes. It afforded the Aryan race with more living space, and it provided the Nazis with a dumping ground for unwanted Jews. Hitler promptly divided Poland into two sections. The western portion, dubbed the Warthegau, was annexed to the Reich. The unincorporated eastern section was called the General Government administered largely by the SS, Hitler's all-powerful police arm of the Nazi state. Its function was to receive the shipments of Jews who had been expelled from Germany and western Poland.

The final three months of 1939 saw thousands of Jews being rounded up and transported by rail to the General Government region. In the process, hundreds of Jewish adults and children died of cold, exposure, or starvation. By this process, one German city after another was declared *Judenfrei*.

But the Nazis' expulsion program for Jews hit a serious snag. Now that over 2 million Jews were resettled in the General Government, what was to be done with them? Hitler's answer was twofold: "Enclose" them inside labor camps and ghettos. In 125 labor camps scattered over Poland, Jewish detainees were forced to dig trenches, clear forests, build roads, drain marshes, and construct new camps.

Other Jews were enclosed in confined sections of the cities called ghettos. Walls or barbed wire fences were constructed to keep Jews inside, isolated from their friends and families. "There was no escape,"

one resident later recalled. "Like cattle we had been herded into the corral, and the gate had been barred behind us."[84] Rations were meager, clothing insufficient, and sickness and overcrowding were rampant. Those who died were often thrown into the streets naked, their clothes hoarded by the living. Ghettoization, however, was also a temporary phase in the Nazi program to rid Europe of Jews.

The Final Solution

Murder had always been part of Hitler's "remedy." As the war opened, he ordered the T-4 euthanasia program, in which nearly one hundred thousand mentally unstable, physically deformed, or incurably ill Germans were killed by lethal injection or poison gas. Beginning in 1941, SS "special action groups" or *Einsatzgruppen*, followed Nazi armies into the Soviet Union, shooting to death an estimated 1.5 million Jewish civilians in the occupied territories.

But nothing could match the fatal efficiency of the extermination camps. In December 1941, the SS under Hitler deputy Heinrich Himmler opened the first Nazi death camp at Chelmno, Poland, for the mass murder of the Jews. While this camp utilized motorized vans that killed with carbon monoxide gas, later camps were equipped with gas chambers and crematoria, large ovens for incinerating the countless corpses. A total of six extermination camps were constructed, the largest of which, Auschwitz, was capable of the murder of up to eight thousand people a day.

The lethal routine seldom varied. The victims—Jews, Slavs, Greeks, Gypsies, and Russians—arrived at a death camp by train, packed into cattle cars. They were ordered to bathe. After undressing, large groups of prisoners were herded into rooms that resembled showers. But when the "showers" were turned on, it was poison gas that spewed out. One SS official recalled:

> At Auschwitz I used Zyklon B, which was a crystallized prussic acid dropped into the death chamber. It took from three to fifteen minutes to kill the people in the chamber, according to climatic conditions. We knew when the people were dead because their screaming stopped. We usually waited about half an hour before we opened the doors and removed the bodies . . . we built our gas chambers to accommodate two thousand people at one time.[85]

Extermination of the "defilers" of Aryan blood in mind-numbing proportions—this was Hitler's Final Solution. The full horrifying scale of Nazi mass murder would not be revealed to the world for several years. It came only at the end of the world conflict which Hitler

A crowded trainload of Jews, Slavs, Gypsies, and others arrives at its grim destination: a Nazi extermination camp.

himself had started—and had predicted so confidently in *Mein Kampf.*

The Death of the Reich

In 1941 Hitler and his Japanese allies made two fatal miscalculations. On June 22 the Führer betrayed his Russian allies by rashly ordering the mass invasion of the Soviet Union. The German Sixth Army attacked Stalingrad but was mired there through the Russian winter, poorly supplied and facing resilient Soviet forces. The Germans' surrender in early 1943 thwarted Hitler's designs on Russia as he had outlined them in *Mein Kampf:* "We stop the endless German movement to the south and west, and turn our gaze toward the land in the east. . . . If we speak of soil in Europe today, we can primarily have in mind only Russia and her vassal border states."[86]

The second miscalculation was the Japanese bombing on the American naval base at Pearl Harbor, Hawaii, on December 7. Roused to action, the United States entered the war. With the American and Russian giants arrayed against Germany, the odds were no longer in its favor.

By early 1944 the tide of the war had turned against the Third Reich. On June 6 American, British, and Canadian troops made a daring landing on the Normandy coast of France and began a steady push inland toward Germany. Meanwhile, the Soviet army was forcing back Nazi troops in the east. In August, Paris was liberated by the Allies. Now there was little to stop them from marching on Germany.

Growing desperate, Hitler ordered an offensive against the approaching U.S. and British armies in December. It failed. In January 1945 the Russians entered Poland and liberated the death camp at Auschwitz. The end was approaching for Hitler and his Nazis, and he knew it. With his mistress and his deputies, the increasingly irrational Führer took refuge in an underground bunker beneath the Nazi Chancellery in Berlin.

By April 25, Soviet troops had the city completely surrounded. Inside the bunker, a resigned Hitler married Eva Braun, his mistress of thirteen years, on April 29. The next afternoon, in Hitler's suite, the Führer and his wife committed suicide. With Hitler's death, the end of the Third Reich was a mere formality. That formality was the unconditional surrender of the German armed forces to the Allies on May 7, 1945.

A German girl is horrified by the sight of murdered Jews, exposed here by Allied troops so that townspeople would be forced to witness the terrible handiwork of their leaders.

"He Offered Us Hope!"

How could Adolf Hitler have risen to such deadly power in Germany? How could the German people ever have rallied behind a man who murdered dissenters in cold blood or starved people in ghettos and concentration camps? What did they see in him?

In his book Why Hitler? *Samuel W. Mitcham Jr. relates an encounter with a man who offered one reason:*

"I once knew a German who was the type of man one would not mind having as a neighbor—just a good, solid, helpful, pleasant sort of fellow who was getting up in years. . . . Certainly, he was not the type of monster who committed murder on such a massive scale in the 1940s. I was appalled when he told me, in a confidential manner, that he had voted for Hitler. After I expressed my shock, he became very thoughtful. He reminisced about being a young man lying in bed next to his wife at night, but neither of them could sleep since their children in the next room were crying because they had not had enough to eat. Then his eyes focused directly on mine. 'Yes,' he declared forcefully, 'you're damn right I voted for Hitler. He offered us hope!'"

The Reality of *Mein Kampf*

Once in his early days as Germany's führer, Hitler claimed to regret having written *Mein Kampf.* Yet it is to history's benefit that he did. With all its crudity, its bigotry, its irrational ravings, *Mein Kampf* provides some of the truest clues we have to the mind and character of Adolf Hitler. Its chapters hint at the makeup of the man whose obsessions and drive changed twentieth-century history.

The hate-inspired tenets of *Mein Kampf* had propelled Hitler forward all of his adult life. In turn, he had fashioned the Nazis into the brutal architects of a "better" Germany. In reality, he succeeded only in bringing down destruction upon the very party he had built, upon the very nation he claimed to revere. It was the only part of the Nazi story that *Mein Kampf* had not foretold.

Aftermath: The Legacy of *Mein Kampf*

"The hallmark of Adolf Hitler's power was destruction," writes biographer Ian Kershaw. "His political 'career' began out of the destruction of the Germany he had until then [1919] identified with. . . . It ended in the far more comprehensive destruction of 'his' Germany through total defeat and devastation in 1945."[87] At the war's end, the people of Europe painfully began taking stock of that destruction. From the dust of the rubble and the stench of the dead a staggering picture of carnage and loss began to take shape.

The Price of War

Exact totals are elusive. Some estimates put the overall death count for World War II as high as 55 million people, both military and civilian. The Soviet Union undoubtedly suffered the greatest loss of life, estimated at 25 million people. Seven million Germans were killed, 13 million Chinese and Japanese. Both the United States and Britain suffered more than four hundred thousand deaths each. France lost over six hundred thousand of her population.

The Holocaust—Hitler's campaign against the Jews and other "undesirables"—left its own legacy of horror. It involved nearly every nation in Europe and cost the widely cited figure of 6 million Jewish lives. Two million of that number perished of starvation, disease, or overwork in the ghettos and labor camps. More than a million died at the hands of the *Einsatzgruppen* and other firing squad actions. Nazi death camps claimed the lives of at least 3 million Jews. Fatalities for other ethnic groups included a half million Gypsies and four million Poles, Russians, Ukrainians, and other Slavic people who were forced into slave labor.

The financial cost of the war, estimated at $1 trillion, impoverished many of the twenty-one nations involved. Germany alone doled out $272 billion, second only to the United States with $341 billion. Even more appalling was the overwhelming devastation visited on Europe by the war. A number of its greatest cities—London, Vienna, Budapest, and Belgrade—were severely damaged. Others, notably Berlin and Warsaw, were nearly obliterated. Countless towns and smaller villages were left in smoking ruins. Splendid buildings and cathedrals dating back to the Middle Ages were leveled, their precious stores of art, ancient books, and artifacts destroyed.

Along with the horrors of physical destruction came the human re-actions of shock, grief, guilt, anger, and a growing desire for ven-geance. "What is Europe now?" wrote British prime minister Winston Churchill sadly. "A rubble heap, a charnel house [structure for receiving the dead], a breeding ground of pestilence and hate."[88]

The New Face of Europe

Inevitably, the upheaval of the war brought sweeping changes to the face of Europe. "State boundaries are made by man and changed by man,"[89] Hitler had written in Volume 2 of *Mein Kampf*. He had as-sumed, of course, that the Nazis would do the changing. But it was Hitler's enemies, not his Reich, who would take on that task.

The outcome of World War II spelled the end of Europe's domi-nance on the world stage. The global primacy she had enjoyed for centuries gave way to an immense shifting of territorial bounda-ries, authority, and position. No longer were Germany, Britain, and France dominant powers in the traditional military sense. That role now belonged to only two countries: the United States and, ironically, the Soviet Union—the very nation Hitler had dreamed of conquering.

Allied soldiers at Buchenwald view the evidence of unspeakable crimes carried out by the millions here and in other Nazi death camps.

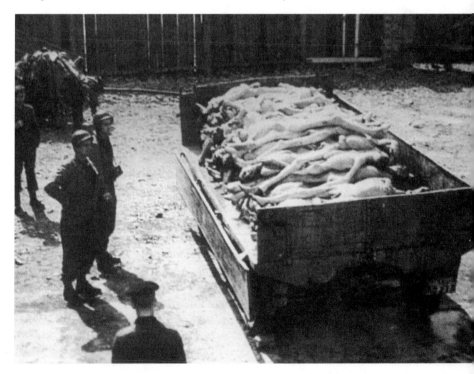

Battered and bloodied, she emerged from the war as the second global superpower, with much of Central and Eastern Europe under her control.

Defeated and demoralized, Germany quickly fell under the victors' knife. The nation was carved into four separate zones, each administered by Soviet, British, French, or American forces. The capital city of Berlin—in the heart of the Soviet zone—was divided in the same fashion. In 1949 the French, British, and American zones of Germany united to become one independent country, the Federal Republic of Germany, or simply, West Germany. The Soviet section was renamed the German Democratic Republic, although it was anything but a democracy. Better known as East Germany, it formed part of the Communist bloc in Europe.

Nazi Horrors Revealed

As American, British, and Russian forces made their final drive on Germany, the full horror of Nazi ruthlessness began to reveal itself. In towns and villages that dotted Poland, France, Austria, and Germany herself, the Allies stumbled upon the labor camps, concentration camps, and death camps long kept secret by the Third Reich. Here they were met by the sight of torture and death in staggering proportions. Inside the barbed wire enclosures, emaciated survivors, hollow-eyed and ghostly, moved like walking corpses about the camp. Others lay helplessly on cots or bunks, only days or hours away from death. The gas chambers were now empty and silent, but the chimneys of some crematoria still belched foul, dark smoke. And then

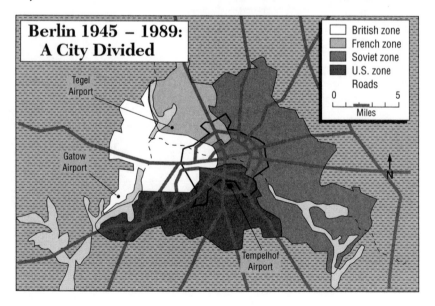

Berlin 1945 – 1989: A City Divided

British zone
French zone
Soviet zone
U.S. zone
Roads
0   5
Miles

Tegel Airport
Gatow Airport
Tempelhof Airport

N

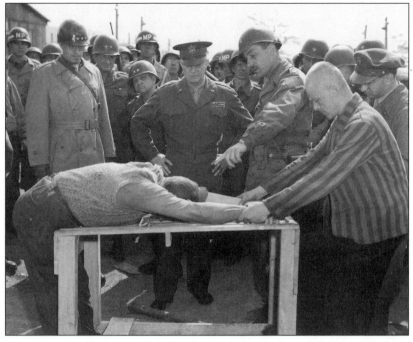

Determined to document the war crimes of the Nazi regime, General Eisen-hower listens intently as concentration camp survivors demonstrate how they were tortured.

there were the dead. A soldier in General George Patton's Third Army related his experiences when American troops arrived at the concentration camp at Buchenwald, Germany:

> No sooner had we passed the barbed wire gate than a nause-ating stench reached our nostrils. But what we saw was even worse. . . . There were dead bodies all around the camp, some lying side by side, others piled upon each other like cord-wood. . . . [Further on] beyond the buildings, was a deep pit. It was filled with naked bodies—men, women and children—in all the grotesque positions of death. Someone said that these dead were Jews.[90]

Recoiling from the sight, General Patton turned from the death pit and retched. General Dwight D. Eisenhower, meanwhile, ordered his staff to take photographs, talk to prisoners, and write down what they were told. He wanted a concrete record of all they saw and heard out of concern that no one would believe the unfathomable vi-ciousness of the Nazis otherwise. Had world leaders ever read *Mein Kampf*, this passage might have made Hitler's intentions a little clearer: "If our people and our state become the victim of these bloodthirsty and avaricious [money-hungry] Jewish tyrants of nations," he had written, "the whole earth will sink into the snares of this octopus; if Germany frees herself from this embrace, this greatest of dangers to nations may be regarded as broken for the whole world."[91] In Auschwitz, Dachau, Bergen-Belsen, and many other camps, the Allies witnessed similar evidence of barbarity, the result of the racist policies outlined in Hitler's Nazi bible.

Still more stunning revelations were to follow. Within months, the victorious Allied nations established the International Military Tribunal in Nuremberg, Germany, to bring surviving Nazi war criminals to trial. The testimony of eyewitnesses and the Nazi defendants uncovered further chilling details of the capture, torture, and murder of the Jews. The years that followed saw a series of further legal actions brought against the Nazi generals and party leaders; indeed, World War II war crimes trials continue to the present day. As recently as July 2002, a German tribunal convicted former SS officer Friedrich Engel for the murder of fifty-nine Italian resistance fighters in 1944. Known at that time as "the Butcher of Genoa," Engel was ninety-three when he was brought to trial.

Hitler's Philosophy Lives On

Unfortunately, the collapse of the Third Reich in 1945 did not mean the end of the Nazi way of thinking. The racist—particularly anti-Semitic—philosophy of Hitler as he set it down in *Mein Kampf* remains tragically alive into the twenty-first century. Despite the obvious and painful lessons learned in the decades since World War II and the Holocaust, Hitler's philosophy still attracts adherents in parts of the United States, South Africa, and Europe.

In 1990, for example, on the usually peaceful campus of the University of Illinois, a group of undergraduates formed a human ring around a fraternity house. "Hitler had the right idea!"[92] they shouted over and over. The building housed a Jewish fraternity.

The New Nazis

The party of Hitler survives today not in large, well-constructed organizations, but in small, far-flung groups with no real connection to each other. These groups are referred to as "neo-Nazis." Like the Führer they idolize, these groups are extremely racist, nationalistic, and sometimes violent. While most neo-Nazis have never read *Mein Kampf*, they nonetheless put many of its tenets into practice. Generally, they despise Jews, black people, homosexuals, and other "undesirables." The world, they insist, was created for the white Christian race to dominate.

Probably the first U.S. neo-Nazi group inspired by the Third Reich was the "Silver Shirts," founded by William Dudley Pelley in 1933. Shortly afterward, former German Fritz Kuhn established the German-American Bund. This organization staged Nazi-inspired parades, and set up paramilitary camps in five different states. Even more successful was the American Nazi Party (ANP), created by

The Nuremberg Trials

While Hitler eluded public reckoning by committing suicide, other Nazi officials survived the war to face their accusers. By the fall of 1945 the Allies were ready to bring the first group of Nazi war criminals to trial. But how were the defendants to be tried, and under what charges? The Allies decided on two existing categories of unlawful acts: "crimes against peace" and "war crimes." To these charges they added two more: "conspiracy" to wage wars of aggression, and "crimes against humanity."

On November 16, 1945, the international tribunal (court) opened its proceedings at the site of Hitler's most spectacular rallies, the city of Nuremberg. Twenty-two former Nazi officials sat in the prisoners' dock to await their fates. Among them were Rudolf Hess (a Hitler deputy who had taken dictation for *Mein Kampf*), Hans Frank (Hitler's attorney and governor-general of Poland), and Nazi foreign minister Joachim von Ribbentrop. The most prominent defendant was Reichsmarschall Hermann Göring, Luftwaffe commander and one of the Reich's most powerful men. Missing from the proceedings were Nazi propaganda minister Joseph Goebbels and SS leader Heinrich Himmler. Both men had committed suicide soon after Hitler's death to avoid the humiliation of prosecution.

For eleven taut months, a shocked world followed the proceedings closely. Under intense questioning by judges from the United States, Britain, France, and the Soviet Union, the Nazi prisoners revealed still more horrifying secrets of Nazi sadism and savagery. Graphic photos, diaries, letters, and eyewitness testimony were presented as evidence. In the end, only three of the original defendants were acquitted. Four were given stiff prison terms, while three more received life imprisonment. A dozen were condemned to death by hanging. Hermann Göring cheated the noose by swallowing a cyanide capsule and dying in his cell.

Twelve more cases were later tried in Nuremberg. In the years that followed, smaller tribunals sat in eight other nations. But it was the city of Nuremberg that became synonymous with judgment on the Nazis.

Neo-Nazis such as this German skinhead perpetuate Hitler's racist agenda.

George Lincoln Rockwell in 1959. A devout anti-Communist, Rockwell had read *Mein Kampf* and adapted its hostile philosophy toward bolshevism to his postwar political movement.

Today, the nation with the highest number of neo-Nazis is Germany. Since the reunification of East and West Germany in 1990, the appearance of neo-Nazi groups has risen dramatically partly in response to large influxes of immigrants from Africa and the Middle East. Violent hate crimes have risen alarmingly.

On June 11, 2000, for example, thirty-nine-year-old Alberto Adriano, a Mozambican immigrant and father of three, was kicked and beaten to death by three white males—one adult and two juveniles—in Dessau, Germany, a murder charged as a crime of hate. In an attempt to counter this trend, the German government approved $35 million to combat racism, and $4.7 million to aid victims of neo-Nazi hate crimes.

Perhaps surprisingly, most of Germany's neo-Nazi literature comes from the United States. The reason: Germany has passed tough laws against hate crimes and deals harshly with groups like the neo-Nazis. The United States, in contrast, has a strong tradition of protecting free speech and freedom of the press. American neo-Nazi organizations

Countering Neo-Nazis in the Courts

On November 13, 1988, Mulugeta Seraw was talking to two friends on his street in Portland, Oregon, when the attack began. Three members of a skinhead group called East Side White Pride approached the young Ethiopian man and knocked him to the ground. Two of the assailants pounded Seraw with their fists. The third struck the Ethiopian's head three times with a baseball bat. Seraw died of a fractured skull six hours later.

The senseless and violent actions of the three attackers, Ken Mieske, Steve Strasser, and Kyle Brewster, outraged the country. At their trial, Mieske admitted to killing Seraw because he was black. Although all three men were found guilty, civil rights attorney Morris Dees believed there was more to the story. Dees was convinced that the three skinheads had been influenced by a larger, organized hate group. He targeted Tom Metzger, founder and leader of the White Aryan Resistance (WAR), a racist neo-Nazi organization. Dees charged that Metzger and his son John had dispatched WAR members to Portland to urge skinheads to harass and attack nonwhite citizens. But instead of going after the Metzgers in a criminal proceeding, Dees took a different route. He brought a wrongful death civil suit against the two on behalf of the Seraw family.

American neo-Nazi Tom Metzger.

Supporting Dees was the Southern Poverty Law Center, a legal center he had founded dedicated to tracking hate groups. After two years of investigations, the case went to trial. The jury agreed that the Metzgers and the WAR were liable for Seraw's death. It ordered a total of $9 million in damages to be paid to the victim's family. The opponents of hate crimes now had a new arena in which to battle those who committed them: the nation's civil courts.

have more freedom to write, print, and distribute pamphlets, newsletters, books, and other materials than their German counterparts.

One tactic of neo-Nazis is to use religion as a front for their bigoted philosophies. One such group takes the name World Church of the Creation (WCOTC). Founded in 1973 by Ben Klassen, a Ukranian immigrant, the WCOTC encourages its members to "gird for total war against the Jews and the . . . mud races of the world."[93] In the 1990s, members of the WCOTC allegedly murdered at least three African Americans, Jews, and Asian Americans, and wounded several more. In wording reminiscent of *Mein Kampf*, the group's website plainly states the WCOTC's creed: "What is good for the White Race is the highest virtue; what is bad for the White Race is the ultimate sin."[94] Other U.S. neo-Nazi organizations include White Aryan Resistance and the Christian Identity.

Skinheads

Within the last thirty years, bands of young people openly flaunting their white supremacist views have joined "skinhead" gangs. With their bald pates or "buzz" haircuts and combat boots, skinheads have attempted to pick up Hitler's fallen banner. The Anti-Defamation League (ADL) has calculated skinhead strength worldwide as 70,000 youths operating in at least thirty-three countries. Germany is home to the most skinheads with an estimated 5,000. It is followed by Hungary and the Czech Republic with 4,000 each, and the United States with 3,500. Skinheads have devised their own subculture partly by listening to racist music and playing violent video games with anti-Semitic themes. Like neo-Nazis in general, they are only loosely organized.

With names like American Frontists, the Fourth Reich, and the Confederate Hammerskins, most skinheads' bands demonstrate a deep anti-Semitism and a penchant for violence, including beatings and murders, church bombings, and arson. Skinhead activity is nonpolitical; it is channeled instead into direct violence. According to ADL estimates, at least twenty-five murders were committed in the United States by skinheads over the decade of the 1990s.

In Lubbock, Texas, for example, a skinhead named Roy Ray Martin and two Hispanic accomplices assaulted three black men in October 1995. One of the victims died of his wounds. The indictment against the three attackers reported they were hoping to "start a revolution or race war"[95] against African Americans. In Martin's house, investigators found a swastika, a photo of Adolf Hitler, and a Nazi flag.

Ironically, the advances in information technology of the last two decades seem to be working in the skinheads's favor. The usual targets of skinheads seeking to recruit more young people to their ranks are

Countering Neo-Nazis in the Community

In 1992 the town of Billings, Montana, stood as a shining example of the power of the individual against organized bigotry. Like many communities, Billings suffered the indignities and outrage of hate crimes against its citizens. In her book, Neo-Nazis: A Growing Threat, *author Kathlyn Gay describes how the citizens banded together to combat the growing problem:*

"As anti-Semitic and racist acts escalated, the community began to organize to prevent violence and to help and support victims of attacks. . . . Labor union members, for example, helped repaint a Native American home that had been damaged by graffiti. After skinheads invaded an African Methodist Episcopal Church to intimidate the congregation, members of predominantly white churches began to attend the African-American church to lend support. When a cement block was thrown through the window of a Jewish home where a Menorah [a ceremonial seven- or nine-branched candelabra used in Jewish religious observances] was being displayed, the local newspaper published a full-page picture of a Menorah. With the encouragement of the newspaper, thousands of Jews and non-Jews displayed the Menorah as a sign of unity. Other signs appeared, declaring, 'Not in Our Town. No Hate.' More and more citizens protested the violence, marched in candlelight vigils, and formed solidarity groups to combat attacks that were linked to skinheads, Aryan Nations, and Klan members. Eventually the city put an end to the series of hate crimes."

white males between the ages of thirteen and twenty. This is also the prime group of users of the Internet. As more and more skinhead and neo-Nazi groups set up websites, they are finding the Internet a likely place to draw more young people into their folds. The twisted theories, prejudices, and self-delusions Hitler laid out in *Mein Kampf* are getting the twenty-first-century treatment. The message of hatred, once tapped out on a borrowed typewriter in Landsberg Prison are even now—some seventy-five years later—wending their way through cyberspace.

The Bitter Harvest of *Mein Kampf*

Barely a month after the death of President Hindenburg in 1934, the new führer attended the Nazi Party Congress in Nuremberg. It seemed as if all Germany was listening as a Nazi official read a new

Adolf Hitler's legacy is one of hatred and racism, death and destruction. The regime he predicted would last a thousand years endures only in the human psyche, as one of the most brutal in history.

proclamation by Hitler to the great flag-draped hall. "The Age of Nerves of the nineteenth century has found its close with us," the document ran. "There will be no other revolution in Germany for the next one thousand years!"[96]

It was this vision of a "thousand-year Reich" that Hitler saw as his legacy to Germany and the world. Yet only twelve years after Hitler's proclamation, Nazi lieutenant Hans Frank—on trial in Nuremberg for war crimes—confessed, "A thousand years will pass and the guilt of Germany will not be erased."[97]

Here was the real legacy of *Mein Kampf.* In trying to reshape the world, Adolf Hitler, blinded by his own rabid hatred, destroyed what he claimed to cherish. In doing so, he changed the fate of his nation, the balance of world power, and the course of twentieth-century history. He had tried to build by destroying, and failed. The final lesson of *Mein Kampf* and Adolf Hitler may be, as Professor Norman Rich has observed, "Out of all the suffering, bloodshed and destruction which Nazism inflicted on the world, the Nazi movement contributed nothing whatever to culture and civilization. Nothing except a terrible lesson about how fragile and vulnerable human civilization is."[98]

Appendix

Excerpts from *Mein Kampf*

From Volume 1, Chapter 2: Years of Study and Suffering in Vienna

After the death of my mother I came to Vienna for the third time. This visit was destined to last several years. Since I had been there before I had recovered my old calm and resoluteness. The former self-assurance had come back, and I had my eyes steadily fixed on the goal. I would be an architect. Obstacles are placed across our path in life, not to be boggled at but to be surmounted. And I was fully determined to surmount these obstacles, having the picture of my father constantly before my mind, who had raised himself by his own efforts to the position of a civil servant though he was the poor son of a village shoemaker. I had a better start, and the possibilities of struggling through were better. At that time my lot in life seemed to me a harsh one; but today I see in it the wise workings of Providence. The Goddess of Fate clutched me in her hands and often threatened to smash me; but the will grew stronger as the obstacles increased, and finally the will triumphed.

I am thankful for that period of my life, because it hardened me and enabled me to be as tough as I now am. And I am even more thankful because I appreciate the fact that I was thus saved from the emptiness of a life of ease and that a mother's darling was taken from tender arms and handed over to Adversity as to a new mother. Though I then rebelled against it as too hard a fate, I am grateful that I was thrown into a world of misery and poverty and thus came to know the people for whom I was afterwards to fight.

It was during this period that my eyes were opened to two perils, the names of which I scarcely knew hitherto and had no notion whatsoever of their terrible significance for the existence of the German people. These two perils were Marxism and Judaism. . . .

Knowledge of the Jews is the only key whereby one may understand the inner nature and therefore the real aims of Social Democracy.

The man who has come to know this race has succeeded in removing from his eyes the veil through which he had seen the aims and meaning of his Party in a false light; and then, out of the murk and fog of social phrases rises the grimacing figure of Marxism.

Today it is hard and almost impossible for me to say when the word 'Jew' first began to raise any particular thought in my mind. I do not remember even having heard the word at home during my father's lifetime. If this name were mentioned in a derogatory sense I think the old gentleman would just have considered those who used it in this way as being uneducated reactionaries. In the course of his career he had come to be more or less a cosmopolitan, with strong views on nationalism, which had its effect on me as well. In school, too, I found no reason to alter the picture of things I had formed at home. . . .

Once, when passing through the Inner City, I suddenly encountered a phenomenon in a long caftan and wearing black side-locks. My first thought was: Is this a Jew? They certainly did not have this appearance in Linz. I watched the man stealthily and cautiously; but the longer I gazed at the strange countenance and examined it feature by feature, the more the question shaped itself in my brain: Is this a German?

As was always my habit with such experiences, I turned to books for help in removing my doubts. For the first time in my life I bought myself some anti-Semitic pamphlets for a few pence. But unfortunately they all began with the assumption that in principle the reader had at least a certain degree of information on the Jewish question or was even familiar with it. Moreover, the tone of most of these pamphlets was such that I became doubtful again, because the statements made were partly superficial and the proofs extraordinarily unscientific. For weeks, and indeed for months, I returned to my old way of thinking. The subject appeared so enormous and the accusations were so far-reaching that I was afraid of dealing with it unjustly and so I became again anxious and uncertain.

Naturally I could no longer doubt that here there was not a question of Germans who happened to be of a different religion but rather that there was question of an entirely different people. For as soon as I began to investigate the matter and observe the Jews, then Vienna appeared to me in a different light. Wherever I now went I saw Jews, and the more I saw of them the more strikingly and clearly they stood out as a different people from the other citizens. Especially the Inner City and the district northwards from the Danube Canal swarmed with a people who, even in outer appearance, bore no similarity to the Germans.

But any indecision which I may still have felt about that point was finally removed by the activities of a certain section of the Jews themselves. A great movement, called Zionism, arose among them. Its aim was to assert the national character of Judaism, and the movement was strongly represented in Vienna.

From Volume 1, Chapter 8: The Beginning of My Political Activities

It is not the business of him who lays down a theoretical programme to explain the various ways in which something can be put into practice. His task is to deal with the problem as such; and, therefore, he has to look to the end rather than the means. The important question is whether an idea is fundamentally right or not. The question of whether or not it may be difficult to carry it out in practice is quite another matter. When a man whose task it is to lay down the principles of a programme or policy begins to busy himself with the question as to whether it is expedient and practical, instead of confining himself to the statement of the absolute truth, his work will cease to be a guiding star to those who are looking about for light and leading and will become merely a recipe for every-day life. The man who lays down the programme of a movement must consider only the goal. It is for the political leader to point out the way in which that goal may be reached. The thought of the former will, therefore, be determined by those truths that are everlasting, whereas the activity of the latter must always be guided by taking practical account of the circumstances under which those truths have to be carried into effect.

The greatness of the one will depend on the absolute truth of his idea, considered in the abstract; whereas that of the other will depend on whether or not he correctly judges the given realities and how they may be utilized under the guidance of the truths established by the former. The test of greatness as applied to a political leader is the success of his plans and his enterprises, which means his ability to reach the goal for which he sets out; whereas the final goal set up by the political philosopher can never be reached; for human thought may grasp truths and picture ends which it sees like clear crystal, though such ends can never be completely fulfilled because human nature is weak and imperfect. The more an idea is correct in the abstract, and, therefore, all the more powerful, the smaller is the possibility of putting it into practice, at least as far as this latter depends on human beings. The significance of a political philosopher does not depend on the practical success of the plans he lays down but rather on their absolute truth and the influence they exert on the progress of mankind. If it were otherwise, the founders of religions could not be considered as the greatest men who have ever lived, because their moral aims will never be completely or even approximately carried out in practice. Even that religion which is called the Religion of Love is really no more than a faint reflex of the will of its sublime Founder. But its significance lies in the orientation which it endeavoured to give to human civilization, and human virtue and morals. . . .

For the greater the work which a man does for the future, the less will he be appreciated by his contemporaries. His struggle will accordingly be all the more severe, and his success all the rarer. When, in the course of centuries, such a man appears who is blessed with success then, towards the end of his days, he may have a faint prevision of his future fame. But such great men are only the Marathon runners of history. The laurels of contemporary fame are only for the brow of the dying hero.

The great protagonists are those who fight for their ideas and ideals despite the fact that they receive no recognition at the hands of their contemporaries. They are the men whose memories will be enshrined in the hearts of the future generations. It seems then as if each individual felt it his duty to make retroactive atonement for the wrong which great men have suffered at the hands of their contemporaries. Their lives and their work are then studied with touching and grateful admiration. Especially in dark days of distress, such men have the power of healing broken hearts and elevating the despairing spirit of a people. . . .

What we have to fight for is the necessary security for the existence and increase of our race and people, the subsistence of its children and the maintenance of our racial stock unmixed, the freedom and independence of the Fatherland; so that our people may be enabled to fulfill the mission assigned to it by the Creator.

From Volume 1, Chapter 11: Race and People

If Nature does not wish that weaker individuals should mate with the stronger, she wishes even less that a superior race should intermingle with an inferior one; because in such a case all her efforts, throughout hundreds of thousands of years, to establish an evolutionary higher stage of being, may thus be rendered futile.

History furnishes us with innumerable instances that prove this law. It shows, with a startling clarity, that whenever Aryans have mingled their blood with that of an inferior race the result has been the downfall of the people who were the standard-bearers of a higher culture. In North America, where the population is prevalently Teutonic, and where those elements intermingled with the inferior race only to a very small degree, we have a quality of mankind and a civilization which are different from those of Central and South America. In these latter countries the immigrants—who mainly belonged to the Latin races—mated with the aborigines, sometimes to a very large extent indeed. In this case we have a clear and decisive example of the effect produced by the mixture of races. But in North America the Teutonic element, which has kept its racial stock pure and did not mix it with any other racial stock, has come to dominate the American Continent and will remain master of it as long as that element does not fall a victim to the habit of adulterating its blood. . . .

The Jew offers the most striking contrast to the Aryan. There is probably no other people in the world who have so developed the instinct of self-preservation as the so-called 'chosen' people. The best proof of this statement is found in the simple fact that this race still exists. Where can another people be found that in the course of the last two thousand years has undergone so few changes in mental outlook and character as the Jewish people? And yet what other people has taken such a constant part in the great revolutions? But even after having passed through the most gigantic catastrophes that have overwhelmed mankind, the Jews remain the same as ever. What an infinitely tenacious will-to-live, to preserve one's kind, is demonstrated by that fact! . . .

He will stop at nothing. His utterly low-down conduct is so appalling that one really cannot be surprised if in the imagination of our people the Jew is pictured as the incarnation of Satan and the symbol of evil. . . .

The ignorance of the broad masses as regards the inner character of the Jew, and the lack of instinct and insight that our upper classes display, are some of the reasons which explain how it is that so many people fall an easy prey to the systematic campaign of falsehood which the Jew carries on.

From Volume 2, Chapter 3: Citizens and Subjects of the State

The People's State will classify its population in three groups: Citizens, subjects of the State, and aliens.

The principle is that birth within the confines of the State gives only the status of a subject. It does not carry with it the right to fill any position under the State or to participate in political life, such as taking an active or passive part in elections. Another principle is that the race and nationality of every subject of the State will have to be proved. A subject is at any time free to cease being a subject and to become a citizen of that country to which he belongs in virtue of his nationality. The only difference between an alien and a subject of the State is that the former is a citizen of another country.

The young boy or girl who is of German nationality and is a subject of the German State is bound to complete the period of school education which is obligatory for every German. Thereby he submits to the system of training which will make him conscious of his race and a member of the folk-community. Then he has to fulfill all those requirements laid down by the State in regard to physical training after he has left school; and finally he enters the army. The training in the army is of a general kind. It must be given to each individual German and will render him competent to fulfill the physical and mental requirements of military service. The rights of citizenship shall be conferred on every young man whose health and character have been certified as good, after having completed his period of military service. This act of inauguration in citizenship shall be a solemn ceremony. And the diploma conferring the rights of citizenship will be preserved by the young man as the most precious testimonial of his whole life. It entitles him to exercise all the rights of a citizen and to enjoy all the privileges attached thereto. For the State must draw a sharp line of distinction between those who, as members of the nation, are the foundation and the support of its existence and greatness, and those who are domiciled in the State simply as earners of their livelihood there.

On the occasion of conferring a diploma of citizenship the new citizen must take a solemn oath of loyalty to the national community and the State. This diploma must be a bond which unites together all the various classes and sections of the nation. It shall be a greater honour to be a citizen of this Reich, even as a street-sweeper, than to be the King of a foreign State.

The citizen has privileges which are not accorded to the alien. He is the master in the Reich. But this high honour has also its obligations. Those who show themselves without personal honour or character, or common criminals, or traitors to the fatherland, can at any time be deprived of the rights of citizenship. Therewith they become merely subjects of the State.

The German girl is a subject of the State but will become a citizen when she marries. At the same time those women who earn their livelihood independently have the right to acquire citizenship if they are German subjects.

From Volume 2, Chapter 4: Personality and the Ideal of the People's State

If the principal duty of the National Socialist People's State be to educate and promote the existence of those who are the material out of which the State is formed, it will not be sufficient to promote those racial elements as such, educate them and finally train them for practical life, but the State must also adapt its own organization to meet the demands of this task.

It would be absurd to appraise a man's worth by the race to which he belongs and at the same time to make war against the Marxist principle, that all men are equal, without being determined to pursue our own principle to its ultimate consequences. If we admit the significance of blood, that is to say, if we recognize the race as the fundamental element on which all life is based, we shall have to apply to the individual the logical consequences of this principle. In general I must estimate the worth of nations differently, on the basis of the different races from which they spring, and I must also differentiate in estimating the worth of the individual within his own race. The principle, that one people is not the same as another, applies also to the individual members of a national community. No one brain, for instance, is equal to another; because the constituent elements belonging to the same blood vary in a thousand subtle details, though they are fundamentally of the same quality.

The first consequence of this fact is comparatively simple. It demands that those elements within the folk-community which show the best racial qualities ought to be encouraged more than the others and especially they should be encouraged to increase and multiply. . . .

A Weltanschauung which repudiates the democratic principle of the rule of the masses and aims at giving this world to the best people—that is, to the highest quality of mankind—must also apply that same aristocratic postulate to the individuals within the folk-community. It must take care that the positions of leadership and highest influence are given to the best men. Hence it is not based on the idea of the majority, but on that of personality. . . .

The destructive workings of Judaism in different parts of the national body can be ascribed fundamentally to the persistent Jewish efforts at undermining the importance of personality among the nations that are their hosts and, in place of personality, substituting the domination of the masses. The constructive principle of Aryan humanity is thus displaced by the destructive principle of the Jews. They become the 'ferment of decomposition' among nations and races and, in a broad sense, the wreckers of human civilization. . . .

In its organization the State must be established on the principle of personality, starting from the smallest cell and ascending up to the supreme government of the country.

There are no decisions made by the majority vote, but only by responsible persons. And the word 'council' is once more restored to its original meaning. Every man in a position of responsibility will have councillors at his side, but the decision is made by that individual person alone.

From Volume 2, Chapter 11: Propaganda and Organization

If a movement proposes to overthrow a certain order of things and construct a new one in its place, then the following principles must be clearly understood and must dominate in the ranks of its leadership: Every movement which has gained its human material must first divide this material into two groups: namely, followers and members.

It is the task of the propagandist to recruit the followers and it is the task of the organizer to select the members.

The follower of a movement is he who understands and accepts its aims; the member is he who fights for them.

The follower is one whom the propaganda has converted to the doctrine of the movement. The member is he who will be charged by the organization to collaborate in winning over new followers from which in turn new members can be formed.

To be a follower needs only the passive recognition of the idea. To be a member means to represent that idea and fight for it. From ten followers one can have scarcely more than two members. To be a follower simply implies that a man has accepted the teaching of the movement; whereas to be a member means that a man has the courage to participate actively in diffusing that teaching in which he has come to believe.

Because of its passive character, the simple effort of believing in a political doctrine is enough for the majority, for the majority of mankind is mentally lazy and timid. To be a member one must be intellectually active, and therefore this applies only to the minority.

Such being the case, the propagandist must seek untiringly to acquire new followers for the movement, whereas the organizer must diligently look out for the best elements among such followers, so that these elements may be transformed into members. The propagandist need not trouble too much about the personal worth of the individual proselytes he has won for the movement. He need not inquire into their abilities, their intelligence or character. From these proselytes, however, the organizer will have to select those individuals who are most capable of actively helping to bring the movement to victory.

From Volume 2, Chapter 14: Germany's Policy in Eastern Europe

Our movement must seek to abolish the present disastrous proportion between our population and the area of our national territory, considering national territory as the source of our maintenance or as a basis of political power. And it ought to strive to abolish the contrast between past history and the hopelessly powerless situation in which we are to-day. In striving for this it must bear in mind the fact that we are members of the highest species of humanity on this earth, that we have a correspondingly high duty, and that we shall fulfil this duty only if we inspire the German people with the racial idea, so that they will occupy themselves not merely with the breeding of good dogs and horses and cats, but also care for the purity of their own blood. . . .

National Socialists must stick firmly to the aim that we have set for our foreign policy; namely, that the German people must be assured the territorial area which is necessary for it to exist on this earth. And only for such action as is undertaken to secure those ends can it be lawful in the eyes of God and our German posterity to allow the blood of our people to be shed once again. Before God, because we are sent into this world with the commission to struggle for our daily bread, as creatures to whom nothing is donated and who must be able to win and hold their position as lords of the earth only through their own intelligence and courage. And this justification must be established also before our German posterity, on the grounds that for each one who has shed his blood the life of a thousand others will be guaranteed to posterity. The territory on which one day our German peasants will be able to bring forth and nourish their sturdy sons will justify the blood of the sons of the peasants that has to be shed to-day. And the statesmen who will have decreed this sacrifice may be persecuted by their contemporaries, but posterity will absolve them from all guilt for having demanded this offering from their people. . . .

State frontiers are established by human beings and may be changed by human beings.

Source Notes

Introduction: A Primer for Hatred

1. Quoted in Brenda Stalcup, ed., *Adolf Hitler.* San Diego: Greenhaven, 2000, pp. 29–30.
2. William L. Shirer, *The Rise and Fall of the Third Reich.* New York: Simon & Schuster, 1960, p. 81.

Chapter 1: A Proud Nation Humbled

3. Quoted in Stefan Lorant, *Sieg Heil! An Illustrated History of Germany from Bismarck to Hitler.* New York: W.W. Norton, 1974, p. 45.
4. Lorant, *Sieg Heil!,* pp. 38–39.
5. Lorant, *Sieg Heil!,* p. 40.
6. Quoted in Barbara Tuchman, *The Guns of August.* New York: Dell, 1963, p. 146.
7. E.J. Feuchtwanger, *From Weimar to Hitler.* New York: St. Martin's, 1993, p. 103.
8. Shirer, *The Rise and Fall of the Third Reich,* p. 57.
9. Lorant, *Sieg Heil!,* p. 73.
10. Adolf Hitler, *Mein Kampf,* trans. Ralph Manheim. Boston: Houghton Mifflin, 1971, pp. 3–4.
11. Hitler, *Mein Kampf,* p. 6.
12. August Kubizek, *The Young Hitler I Knew,* trans. E.V. Anderson. Boston: Houghton Mifflin, 1954, p. 54.
13. Hitler, *Mein Kampf,* p. 17.
14. Hitler, *Mein Kampf,* p. 20.
15. Hitler, *Mein Kampf,* pp. 21–22.
16. Hitler, *Mein Kampf,* p. 56.
17. Hitler, *Mein Kampf,* p. 22.
18. Quoted in Shirer, *The Rise and Fall of the Third Reich,* p. 12.
19. Quoted in John Toland, *Adolf Hitler.* New York: Anchor Books, 1976, p. 46.
20. Hitler, *Mein Kampf,* p. 161.
21. Quoted in Toland, *Adolf Hitler,* p. 61.
22. Ian Kershaw, *Hitler: 1889–1936 Hubris.* New York: W.W. Norton, 1999, p. 87.
23. Hitler, *Mein Kampf,* p. 204.

24. Alan Bullock, *Hitler: A Study in Tyranny.* New York: HarperPerennial, 1991, p. 54.

25. Hitler, *Mein Kampf*, pp. 222–24.

26. Hitler, *Mein Kampf*, p. 355.

27. Hitler, *Mein Kampf*, p. 369.

28. Hitler, *Mein Kampf*, p. 492.

29. Kershaw, *Hitler: 1889–1936 Hubris*, p. 153.

Chapter 2: The Nazi Bible: *Mein Kampf*

30. Shirer, *The Rise and Fall of the Third Reich*, p. 62.

31. Quoted in Shirer, *The Rise and Fall of the Third Reich*, p. 68.

32. Shirer, *The Rise and Fall of the Third Reich*, p. 75.

33. Kershaw, *Hitler: 1889–1936 Hubris*, pp. 214–15.

34. Quoted in Shirer, *The Rise and Fall of the Third Reich*, pp. 75–76.

35. Quoted in Shirer, *The Rise and Fall of the Third Reich*, p. 78.

36. Quoted in Toland, *Adolf Hitler*, p. 191.

37. Quoted in Toland, *Adolf Hitler*, p. 196.

38. Quoted in Werner Maser, *Hitler's Mein Kampf: An Analysis*, trans. R.H. Barry. London: Faber and Faber, 1970, p. 23.

39. Hitler, *Mein Kampf*, vii.

40. Joachim C. Fest, *Hitler*, trans. Richard Winston and Clara Winston. San Diego: Harcourt Brace, 1974, p. 202.

41. Hitler, *Mein Kampf*, p. vii.

42. Quoted in Toland, *Adolf Hitler*, p. 201.

43. Quoted in Toland, *Adolf Hitler*, p. 212.

44. Fest, *Hitler*, p. 215.

45. Konrad Heiden, introduction to *Mein Kampf*, by Adolf Hitler, p. xv.

46. Quoted in Robert G. Waite, *The Psychopathic God: Adolf Hitler.* New York: BasicBooks, 1977, pp. 95–96.

47. Quoted in Waite, *The Psychopathic God*, p. 94.

48. Quoted in Waite, *The Psychopathic God*, p. 96.

49. Toland, *Hitler*, p. 46.

50. Quoted in Shirer, *The Rise and Fall of the Third Reich*, p. 39.

51. Hitler, *Mein Kampf*, p. 687.

52. Quoted in Samuel W. Mitcham Jr., *Why Hitler? The Genesis of the Nazi Reich.* Westport, CT: Praeger, 1996, p. 82.

53. Bullock, *Hitler: A Study in Tyranny*, p. 807.

Chapter 3: Seeds of Evil

54. Yehuda Bauer, *A History of the Holocaust.* Danbury, CT: Franklin Watts, 1982, p. 7.

55. Quoted in Bauer, *A History of the Holocaust,* p. 8.

56. Quoted in Bauer, *A History of the Holocaust,* pp. 8–9.

57. Quoted in Bauer, *A History of the Holocaust,* p. 9.

58. Mitcham, *Why Hitler?,* p. 80.

59. Bauer, *A History of the Holocaust,* p. 41.

60. Mitcham, *Why Hitler?,* p. 83.

61. Hitler, *Mein Kampf,* p. 679.

62. Hitler, *Mein Kampf,* p. 134.

63. Hitler, *Mein Kampf,* p. 383.

64. Shirer, *The Rise and Fall of the Third Reich,* p. 90.

65. Robert Payne, *The Life and Death of Adolf Hitler.* New York: Praeger, 1973, p. 197.

66. Lucy S. Dawidowicz, *The War Against the Jews: 1933–1945.* New York: Bantam Books, 1986, p. 143.

67. Mark Arnold-Forster, *The World at War.* New York: The New American Library, 1974, p. 13.

68. Hitler, *Mein Kampf,* p. 681.

Chapter 4: Implementing a National Policy of Hatred

69. Shirer, *The Rise and Fall of the Third Reich,* pp. 111–12.

70. Quoted in Bullock, *Hitler: A Study in Tyranny,* p. 130.

71. Shirer, *The Rise and Fall of the Third Reich,* p. 112.

72. Quoted in Klaus P. Fischer, *Nazi Germany: A New History.* New York: Continuum, 1995, p. 234.

73. Hitler, *Mein Kampf,* p. 449.

74. Quoted in Shirer, *The Rise and Fall of the Third Reich,* p. 194.

75. Hitler, *Mein Kampf,* p. 449.

76. Hitler, *Mein Kampf,* p. 632.

77. Shirer, *The Rise and Fall of the Third Reich,* p. 284.

78. Hitler, *Mein Kampf,* pp. 300, 324.

79. Hitler, *Mein Kampf,* p. 65.

80. Quoted in Amy Newman, *The Nuremberg Laws: Institutionalized Anti-Semitism.* San Diego: Lucent Books, 1999, p. 32.

81. Toland, *Adolf Hitler,* p. 231.

82. Hitler, *Mein Kampf,* p. 139.

83. Hitler, *Mein Kampf,* p. 654.

84. Quoted in Ann Byers, *The Holocaust Overview.* Springfield, NJ: Enslow, 1998, p. 73.

85. Quoted in Bullock, *Hitler: A Study in Tyranny,* p. 701.

86. Hitler, *Mein Kampf,* p. 654.

Chapter 5: Aftermath: The Legacy of *Mein Kampf*

87. Kershaw, *Hitler.* London: Longman, 1991, p. 188.

88. Quoted in Douglas Botting and Editors of Time-Life Books, *The Aftermath: Europe.* Alexandria, VA: Time-Life Books, 1983, p. 23.

89. Hitler, *Mein Kampf,* p. 653.

90. Quoted in Linda Jacobs Altman, *The Holocaust, Hitler and Nazi Germany.* Berkeley Heights, NJ: Enslow, 1999, pp. 5–6.

91. Hitler, *Mein Kampf,* p. 623.

92. Quoted in Kathlyn Gay, *Neo-Nazis: A Growing Threat.* Springfield, NJ: Enslow, 1997, p. 21.

93. "Little White Book, Chapter 24," World Church of the Creator, www.wcotc.com.

94. Matt Hale, "Creator Membership Manual," World Church of the Creator, www.wcotc.com.

95. Quoted in Deborah Able, *Hate Groups.* Berkeley Heights, NJ: Enslow, 2000, p. 194.

96. Quoted in Shirer, *The Rise and Fall of the Third Reich,* p. 230.

97. Quoted in William W. Lace, *Hitler and the Nazis.* San Diego: Lucent Books, 2000, p. 93.

98. Norman Rich, *Hitler's War Aims: The Establishment of the New Order.* New York: W.W. Norton, 1974, p. 426.

For Further Reading

Linda Jacobs. Altman, *The Holocaust, Hitler and Nazi Germany.* Berkeley Heights, NJ: Enslow, 1999. An easy-to-read overview of the years of Nazi persecution of the Jews. Also features background on Adolf Hitler and his regime.

Eleanor H. Ayer, *The Importance of Adolf Hitler.* San Diego: Lucent Books, 1996. Part of Lucent's The Importance of . . . series, this volume examines Hitler's background, early days, influences, rise to power, and fall to defeat and death. Written in an engaging style with plenty of black-and-white illustrations and maps.

Ann Byers, *The Holocaust Overview.* Springfield, NJ: Enslow, 1998. A broad view of the Holocaust for younger readers, thoroughly researched, thoughtfully written, and well illustrated.

R.G. Grant, *Racism: Changing Attitudes 1900–2000.* Austin, TX: Raintree Steck-Vaughn, 2000. A brief and well-illustrated survey of racism across the globe over the last century.

William W. Lace, *Hitler and the Nazis.* San Diego: Lucent Books, 2000. A well-researched, well-written account of the rise and demise of the Führer and the party he did so much to create and destroy. Illustrated with photos and maps.

Earle Rice Jr., *The Final Solution.* San Diego: Lucent Books, 1998. A volume in Lucent's Holocaust Library series, the author describes the causes and the events leading up to and encompassing the Jews' terrible fate at the hands of the Nazis. Black-and-white illustrations.

William L. Shirer, *The Rise and Fall of Adolf Hitler.* New York: Random House, 1961. In this shorter volume tailored to young people, the author of *The Rise and Fall of the Third Reich* retells the story of the Führer's ascent to power, the Reich at war, and the eventual destruction of his Nazi Party.

Editors of Time-Life Books, *Storming to Power.* Alexandria, VA: Time-Life Books, 1989. Profusely illustrated with both black-and-white and color photos, political cartoons, and posters, this volume from Time-Life's Third Reich series focuses on the Nazis' rise to prominence and features a concise text and informative captions.

Works Consulted

Books

Deborah Able, *Hate Groups.* Berkeley Heights, NJ: Enslow, 2000. Part of the Issues in Focus series. A broad yet effective survey of discrimination, racism, and hate groups from a historical standpoint.

Mark Arnold-Forster, *The World at War.* New York: The New American Library, 1974. The companion book to the 1973 British television series, this is a compact, readable history of the Second World War. Illustrated with sixteen pages of photographs.

Yehuda Bauer, *A History of the Holocaust.* Danbury, CT: Franklin Watts, 1982. A classic study of the history of the Jewish people, of world anti-Semitism, and of the fate of European Jewry at the hands of Hitler and the Nazis. Includes numerous maps and charts.

Douglas Botting and Editors of Time-Life Books, *The Aftermath: Europe.* Alexandria, VA: Time-Life Books, 1983. A large-format book that follows the Time-Life formula of generous numbers of striking photographs accompanied by a concise text and informative captions.

Alan Bullock, *Hitler: A Study in Tyranny.* New York: Harper Perennial, 1991. Originally published in 1964, this work is considered by many scholars to be the definitive biography of Adolf Hitler.

Lucy S. Dawidowicz, *The War Against the Jews: 1933–1945.* New York: Bantam Books, 1986. The acclaimed account of the Holocaust by a professor of Jewish history, written with a calm even-handedness. The volume includes chapters on Hitler's life and view of Jews, and anti-Semitism in modern Germany.

Joachim C. Fest, *Hitler.* Trans. Richard Winston and Clara Winston. San Diego: Harcourt Brace, 1974. A weighty but thorough view of the Third Reich and its leader by a respected German journalist.

E.J. Feuchtwanger, *From Weimar to Hitler.* New York: St. Martin's, 1993. A somewhat scholarly but very informative study of German political history and the Weimar Republic's rise and fall, coinciding with Hitler's rise.

Klaus P. Fischer, *Nazi Germany: A New History.* New York: Continuum, 1995. A painstakingly researched and detailed look at the creation, workings, and downfall of the Third Reich by a German historian.

Kathlyn Gay, *Neo-Nazis: A Growing Threat.* Springfield, NJ: Enslow, 1997. Part of the Issues in Focus series. A sobering look at the neo-Nazi phenomenon as it has grown, spread, and evolved since World War II, with background on the Ku Klux Klan as well as the Nazi Party.

Adolf Hitler, *Mein Kampf.* Trans. Ralph Manheim. Boston: Houghton Mifflin, 1971. Paperback edition containing both volumes of the Führer's "Nazi Bible." Verbose, rambling, and at times ranting, it is nonetheless an intriguing look into the beliefs, prejudices, and sinister ambitions of the figure one U.S. journalist has called "the worst man in history."

Eberhard Jackel, *Hitler in History.* Hanover, NH: University Press of New England, 1984. Composed largely of a series of lectures for Brandeis University, this book includes chapters on how Hitler came to power and how he strove to implement his goals.

Ian Kershaw, *Hitler.* London: Longman, 1991. A condensation of noted Hitler biographer Kershaw's university lectures on the Führer, with an interesting and insightful perspective.

Ian Kershaw, *Hitler: 1889–1936 Hubris.* New York: W.W. Norton, 1999. One of the most recent full-length biographies of the man and his times, this volume covers his youth and rise to power. Thorough and engagingly written.

August Kubizek, *The Young Hitler I Knew.* Trans. E.V. Anderson. Boston: Houghton Mifflin, 1954. A different view of the Nazi dictator: his youth as described by a (and possibly the only) childhood friend. Easy to read, and illustrated with photos and sketches.

Stefan Lorant, *Sieg Heil! An Illustrated History of Germany from Bismarck to Hitler.* New York: W.W. Norton, 1974. An accessible, large-format volume featuring scores of black-and-white photos, documents, and political cartoons.

Werner Maser, *Hitler's Mein Kampf: An Analysis.* Trans. R.H. Barry. London: Faber and Faber, 1970. The first of the two sections of this work covers origins and background of Hitler's infamous book; the second examines its content.

Samuel W. Mitcham Jr., *Why Hitler? The Genesis of the Nazi Reich.* Westport, CT: Praeger, 1996. A thoughtful look at the beginnings of the Nazi regime and how Hitler fashioned himself into the leader the German people thought they wanted.

Don Nardo, ed., *The Rise of Nazi Germany.* San Diego: Green-haven, 1999. A wide-ranging selection of essays on various aspects of the Third Reich's origins, birth, and downfall. Includes articles on German youth, education, and women's roles during this period.

Amy Newman, *The Nuremberg Laws: Institutionalized Anti-Semitism.* San Diego: Lucent Books, 1999. The story of the creation of the Nuremberg Laws of 1935, which in effect legalized the persecution of the Jews in Nazi Germany. Includes historical background of the laws and a look at their continuing influence today. Illustrated with photos and diagrams.

Robert Payne, *The Life and Death of Adolf Hitler.* New York: Praeger, 1973. Another lengthy, thorough, yet readable biography of the creator of the Third Reich. This one features some especially interesting appendixes, such as the text of a Hitler letter as a soldier on the western front, excerpts from Eva Braun's diary, and the Führer's final political testament. Illustrated with two sections of photographs and drawings.

Laurence Rees, *The Nazis: A Warning from History.* New York: New Press, 1997. Companion book to the BBC documentary. An interesting view of the Nazi regime, utilizing more than fifty interviews from eyewitnesses. Well illustrated with a number of seldom-seen black-and-white and color photographs.

Norman Rich, *Hitler's War Aims: The Establishment of the New Order.* New York: W.W. Norton, 1974. This work takes a close look at the Führer's plans for his intended war of conquest.

William L. Shirer, *The Rise and Fall of the Third Reich.* New York: Simon & Schuster, 1960. The classic history of Hitler and the Nazi Party by an award-winning journalist who observed much of this history firsthand. Discusses Hitler's rise, the writing of *Mein Kampf*, the death of the Weimar Republic, Germany's role in World War II, and the fall of the Reich.

Brenda Stalcup, ed., *Adolf Hitler.* San Diego: Greenhaven, 2000. A collection of essays on the Nazi leader, composed of excerpts from the books of historians and Hitler scholars. Well organized and informative.

John Toland, *Adolf Hitler.* New York: Anchor Books, 1976. A lengthy, detailed, yet highly readable biography of "that Austrian corporal" with ambitions of world conquest. Well illustrated with photographs.

Barbara Tuchman, *The Guns of August.* New York: Dell, 1963. The acclaimed and engrossing account of the turbulent days leading up to World War I, which created lasting divisions in Europe and which set the stage for the rise of the Nazi Party.

Robert G. Waite, *The Psychopathic God: Adolf Hitler.* New York: BasicBooks, 1977. An intriguing view of the mind, influences, and attitudes of Hitler. The work includes an examination of the remarkable effect the Führer had on the thinking of the German people.

Website

World Church of the Creator (www.wcotc.com). Founded in 1973, the Illinois-based World Church of the Creator espouses neo-Nazi ideals and advocates violent anti-Semitism, racism, and other hate crimes. Its current leader, Matt Hale, cites *Mein Kampf* as an early influence in his conversion to National Socialism.

Index

Central Powers, 24
Chamberlain, Neville, 54
Chaplin, Charlie, 8
Chelmno, Poland, 72
Chinese, 76
Christianity
  Crusades and, 48
  Great War and, 50
  hatred of Jews and, 45–50
  neo-Nazis and, 80
  Protestantism and, 47
Churchill, Winston
  Mein Kampf and, 54
  on outcome of World War II, 77
Communist Party, 61
Communists
  Bolshevic Revolution and, 24
  conspiracy against Germany and, 25
  fire at Reichstag and, 63
  Jews and, 56
  uprisings in Germany by, 15
Compiègne, France, 14
Confederate Hammerskins, 84
Coughlin, Father Charles E., 56
Croatia, 12
Czechoslovakia
  Austria-Hungary and, 12
  invasion of, 69
Czech Republic, 84
Czerny, Josef, 36

Dachau (extermination camp), 80
Darwin, Charles, 4
Dawidowicz, Lucy S.
  on anti-Semitism and Martin Luther, 47
Dees, Morris, 83
Der Völkischer Kurier (newspaper)
  on Hitler's imprisonment, 32
Dessau, Germany, 82
Drexler, Anton, 41

Eastern Europe, 78
Ebert, Friedrich, 16
Eckart, Dietrich, 41
Eisenhower, Dwight D., 79
Enabling Act, 63
England. *See* Great Britain
Engle, Friedrich, 80

Europe
  conflicts in, 12
  Jews in, 49
  neo-Nazis in, 80
  after World War II, 77
  see also Central Europe; Eastern Europe; *names of specific countries*
  extermination camps, 72
  liberation of, 78–80

Fascist Party (Fasci di Combattimento), 57
Federal Republic of Germany (West Germany), 78
Fest, Joachim C.
  on Hitler's motives for writing *Mein Kampf*, 33
  on *Mein Kampf*, 36
Feuchtwanger, E.J.
  on barring of Germany becoming a world power, 14
  on Hitler's description of World War I battle, 13
Final Solution, 72
Finland, 64
First Reich, 10
Four and a Half Years of Struggle Against Lies, Stupidity and Cowardice (Adolf Hitler), 33
Fourth Reich, 84
France
  anti-Semitism in, 49, 56
  declaration of war against Germany by, 14, 70
  Fascist movements in, 57
  fear of Germany by, 12
  German expansion into, 43, 68, 70
  World War II casualties from, 76
Franco-German War of 1870–1871, 19
Frank, Hans, 86
Franz Eher Verlag, 32
Franz Ferdinand (archduke), 14
Frederick III, 10–11
Frederick the Great, 8
Freinberg (hill), 21
From Weimar to Hitler (Feuchtwanger), 13

Führer Principle, 62

Gay, Kathlyn
    on anti-neo-Nazi movement in
        Billings, Montana, 85
General Government, 71
German-American Bund, 81
German Democratic Republic (East
    Germany), 78
German High Command, 14
German Sudetenland, 69
German Workers' Party (DAP),
    24–26, 41
Germany
    agreement with Hitler's philosophy
        for, 44
    alliance with Austria-Hungary and, 14
    arts and anti-Semitism in, 51, 66
    democratic republic of, 15–16
    economic turmoil in, 16, 61
    emotions of, after World War II, 8
    empire of, 10
    fear of Nazi regime, 69
    financial punishment for World
        War I, 14–15
    freedoms during Second Reich of,
        11–12
    gradual erosion of freedoms in, 63,
        68
    Hitler's reunification of, 69
    as industrial giant, 12
    nationalist ambitions of, 28
    neo-Nazis in, 82
    partitioning of, 78
    reaction of, to Treaty of Versailles, 16
    rearming of, 64–65
    reunification and, 82
    social makeup of, 11
    unconditional surrender of, 74–75
    World War II casualties from, 76
Goebbels, Joseph, 66, 81
Göring, Hermann
    air strikes against Britain, 70
    Beer Hall Putsch and, 28
    suicide of, 81
Götterdämmerung (opera), 42
Graf, Ulrich, 28
Great Britain
    anti-Semitism in, 56
    attempted demoralization of, 70

declaration of war against Germany
    by, 14, 70
Normandy invasion and, 73
supremacy of the seas and, 12
World War II casualties from, 76
Great Depression
    effect of, on radical German politics,
        61
    German anti-Semitism and, 54
    Nazi Party and, 68
Great War of 1914–1918, 9
    see also World War I
Greeks, 72
Grey, Sir Edward
    on World War I, 14
Gypsies, 72, 76

Hagen (mythical hero), 51
Hall of Mirrors (Versailles), 16
Hanfstängl, Ernst, 36
Harrer, Karl, 41
Hegel, Georg, 37
Heiden, Konrad
    on Hitler's frankness in Mein
        Kampf, 37
    on obscurity of Hitler, 55
Hemmrich, Franz, 35
Hess, Rudolf
    Beer Hall Putsch and, 28
    editing of Mein Kampf by, 36
    Hitler introduced to, 41
    Nuremberg Trials and, 81
    typing of Mein Kampf by, 33–34
Himmler, Heinrich, 81
Hindenburg, Paul von, 63
    Hitler's rise after death of, 65, 85
    naming of Hitler as chancellor of
        Germany, 62
    story told to National Assembly by, 16
    Weimar government and, 61
History of the Holocaust, A (Bauer), 47
Hitler, Adolf
    abolition of political parties by, 63
    arrest of, 30
    birth of, 17
    death of, 74
    death of mother, 22
    definition of relationship between
        superman vs. subhuman peoples
        by, 65–66

discovers oratory ability, 26
early youth of, 19–20
effect of World War I on, 13, 17, 23
failure of world leaders to take
    seriously, 54
failures in Vienna, 22–23
forbidden to speak publicly, 60
formation of racist and national
    beliefs, 23, 38
as Führer of Nazi Party, 27
as German savior, 10
goals of, 9
grooming for leadership of Nazis,
    41–42
hatred for Social Democratic Party,
    39
Hindenburg and, 62
joining of DAP by, 25–26
on lebensraum, 43
military service of, 13, 23
move to Munich, 23
passions of, 20–21
physical description of, 8
on principle of despotic rule, 62
speech on German unification, 26
strength of resolve of, 28, 61
use of Luther to justify anti-
    Semitism, 47
using trial as a pulpit, 31–32
worship of Wagner, 51
Hitler, Alois, Sr. (father), 18
Hitler, Klara Pölzt (mother), 18–19
Hitler Youth (Hitlerjugend), 68
Holland, 64
Holocaust, 76
Holy Roman Empire, 10
Hungary, 84

Il Duce. *See* Mussolini, Benito
International Military Tribunal, 80
Islam, 48
Italy
    fascism in, 57
    Versailles treaty and, 14

Japan
    Fascist movements in, 57
    as Hitler's allies, 73
    World War II casualties from, 76
Jesus, 45

Jews
    Christian crusaders and, 48–49
    communism and, 25, 50–52
    differentness of, 46
    in Europe, 49, 54, 56
    expulsion program of, 71
    Final Solution and, 39, 54, 72
    forced retirement of, 66
    Four-Year Plan and, 67
    hatred for, 36, 41, 44
    Middle Ages and, 45–46
    money and, 50
    one-day boycott of, 66
    pogroms against, 48
    as scapegoat for Great War, 52
    as threat to Aryan race, 53
Junkers of Prussia, 24

Kahr, Gustav von, 28
Kershaw, Ian
    on Hitler as a soldier, 23
    on Hitler's hallmark of destruction,
        76
    on limited appeal of Hitler early
        on, 27
Klassen, Ben, 84
Kriemhild (mythical hero), 51
Kubizek, August
    on Hitler's discovery of desire for
        leadership and power, 21
    on Hitler's idleness, 20
Kuhn, Fritz, 81
Ku Klux Klan, 56, 85

Landsberg am Lech, Germany, 34
Landsberg Prison, 59
    description of Hitler's cell at, 8
    Hitler's stay at, 32–35
Law for the Removal of the Distress
    of People and State, 63
Law of Protection of German Blood
    and German Honor, 66
League of Nations, 15
lebensraum (living space), 26, 43, 68
Lech River, 34
Liebenfels, Jörg Lanz von
    on racial purity, 39–41
Life and Death of Adolf Hitler, The
    (Payne), 54
List, Guido von, 37–38

St. John Chrysostom, 45
Storm Detachment (Sturmabteilung
 or SA), 26
Strasser, Steve, 83
Sudentenland (Czechoslovakia), 43
swastika (Hakenkreuz), 27, 38

T-4 euthanasia program, 72
Third Reich, 8–9
 Americans and Russians turn
  against, 73
 beginning of, 10, 64
 making *Judenfrei*, 66
 popularity of works of Martin
  Luther during, 47
 world changes and, 9
Toland, John
 on fellow soldiers' view of Hitler, 13
 on lebensraum and Jewish menace,
  68
 on life at Landsberg Prison, 35
 on *Mein Kampf*, 55
 on *Ostara* stirring fears of Jewish
  power, 40–41
Treaty of Versailles
 German guilt and, 14
 German heritage and, 16
 League of Nations and, 15
Tristan und Isolde (Wagner), 42
Trotsky, Leon, 51

Ukrainians, 76
United States, 12
 anti-Semitism in, 56
 entry into World War I by, 14
 neo-Nazis and, 80, 82
 Normandy invasion and, 73
 power after World War II and, 77
 racism in, 56–57
 skin heads in, 84
 World War II casualties from, 76
 see also U.S. Congress
University of Illinois, 80
U.S. Congress, 15

Verdun (fortress), 14

Vienna
 Hitler's days in, 22–23
 hotbed of individual political
  thought, 37
Völkischer Beobachter (Nazi
 newspaper)
 Hitler's articles for, 55, 61
 naming of editor of, 42

Wagner, Richard
 anti-Semitism and, 51, 42
 Hitler's passion for, 20
War Against the Jews, The
 (Dawidowicz), 47
Weimar, Germany, 15
Weimar Republic
 defeat of, 64
 failures of, 28, 52, 68
 fragmentation of, 24
White Aryan Resistance (WAR), 83
Whittenberg, Germany, 47
Why Hitler? (Mitcham) , 46–47
Wilhelm I (kaiser), 10, 17
Wilhelm II (kaiser), 11
 declaration of war against France,
  Great Britain, and Russia by, 14
 dream of domination by, 12
 exile to Holland, 15
Will to Power, The (Nietzsche), 42
Wilson, Woodrow, 15
World at War, The (Arnold-Foster)
 on Mussolini's philosophy, 57
World Church of the Creation
 (WCOTC), 84
World War I, 41
 beginning and end of, 14
 Hitler and, 13, 23–24
 Jews as scapegoat for, 49
 Mussolini during, 57
World War II
 beginning of, 70
 cost of, 76
 end of, 73–74
 Hitler's prediction of, 43
 sales of *Mein Kampf* and, 60
 seed of Nazis and, 61

Picture Credits

Cover photo: © Bettmann/CORBIS
© Associated Press, AP, 8, 58, 82, 83
© Bettmann/CORBIS, 50
Bundesarchiv, courtesy of USHMM Photo Archives, 32
© CORBIS, 19, 40
© Hulton-Deutsch Collection/CORBIS, 17, 20
© Hulton/Archive by Getty Images, 9, 11, 15, 24, 25, 27, 29,
    30, 33, 36, 42, 46, 48, 56, 63, 65, 70, 73, 77, 86
Library of Congress, 22, 62, 79
National Archives, courtesy of USHMM Photo Archives, 74
New York Times Paris Bureau Collection (USIA), 53
United States Holocaust Memorial Museum, 67

About the Author

Writer Duane Damon has a particular interest in American and twentieth-century history. He is the author of *When This Cruel War Is Over: The Civil War Home Front* (1996), *Headin' for Better Times: The Arts of the Great Depression* (2002), and *Growing Up in the Civil War, 1861 to 1865* (2003). He has a son, Drew, and a daughter, Sarah, and lives in Lutz, Florida. This is his first book for Lucent Books.

Damon, Duane.

Mein Kampf.

10/03

$27.45

DATE		

BAKER & TAYLOR